TEACHING
SOCCER

Steps to Success

Joseph A. Luxbacher, PhD
University of Pittsburgh

Leisure Press
Champaign, Illinois

Library of Congress Cataloging-in-Publication Data

Luxbacher, Joe.
  Teaching soccer : steps to success / Joseph Luxbacher.
    p.   cm. -- (Steps to success activity series)
  Includes bibliographical references (p.).
  ISBN 0-88011-392-8
  1. Soccer--Study and teaching.   2. Soccer--Coaching I. Title.
  II. Series.
  GV943.L89   1991
  796.334'2--dc20   90-28870
                                                          CIP

ISBN: 0-88011-392-8

Series Editor: Judy Patterson Wright, PhD
Developmental Editor: June I. Decker, PhD
Managing Editor: Robert King
Assistant Editors: Elizabeth Bridgett, Valerie Hall, and Kari Nelson
Copyeditor: Robert King
Proofreader: Karin Leszczynski
Production Director: Ernie Noa
Typesetters: Brad Colson and Kathy Boudreau-Fuoss
Text Design: Keith Blomberg
Text Layout: Tara Welsch
Cover Design: Jack W. Davis
Cover Photo: Bill Morrow
Line Drawings: Raneé Rogers
Field Diagrams: Gretchen Walters
Printer: United Graphics

Instructional Designer for the Steps to Success Activity Series: Joan N. Vickers, EdD, University of Calgary, Calgary, Alberta, Canada

Leisure Press books are available at special discounts for bulk purchase for sales promotions, premiums, fund-raising, or educational use. Special editions or book excerpts can also be created to specification. For details, contact the Special Sales Manager at Leisure Press.

Printed in the United States of America

10 9 8 7 6 5 4 3 2 1

Leisure Press
A Division of Human Kinetics Publishers, Inc.
Box 5076, Champaign, IL 61825-5076
1-800-747-4457

Canada Office:
Human Kinetics Publishers, Inc.
P.O. Box 2503, Windsor, ON N8Y 4S2
1-800-465-7301 (in Canada only)

UK Office:
Human Kinetics Publishers (UK) Ltd.
P.O. Box 18
Rawdon, Leeds LS19 6TG
England
(0532) 504211

Contents

Series Preface

The Steps to Success Activity Series is a breakthrough in skill instruction through the development of complete learning progressions—the *steps to success*. These *steps* help students quickly perform basic skills successfully and prepare them to acquire advanced skills readily. At each step, students are encouraged to learn at their own pace and to integrate their new skills into the total action of the activity, which motivates them to achieve.

The unique features of the Steps to Success Activity Series are the result of comprehensive development—through analyzing existing activity books, incorporating the latest research from the sport sciences, and consulting with students, instructors, teacher educators, and administrators. This groundwork pointed out the need for three different types of books—for participants, instructors, and teacher educators—were needed. Together these books comprise the Steps to Success Activity Series.

The *participant's book* for each activity is a self-paced, step-by-step guide; learners can use it as a primary resource for a beginning activity class or as a self-instructional guide. The unique features of each *step* in the participant's book include

- sequential illustrations that clearly show proper technique for all basic skills,
- helpful suggestions for detecting and correcting errors,
- excellent drill progressions with accompanying *Success Goals* for measuring performance, and
- a complete checklist for each basic skill for a trained observer to rate the learner's technique.

A comprehensive *instructor's guide* accompanies the participant's book for each activity, emphasizing how to individualize instruction. Each *step* of the instructor's guide promotes successful teaching and learning with

- teaching cues (*Keys to Success*) that emphasize fluidity, rhythm, and wholeness,

- criterion-referenced rating charts for evaluating a participant's initial skill level,
- suggestions for observing and correcting typical errors,
- tips for group management and safety,
- ideas for adapting every drill to increase or decrease the difficulty level,
- quantitative evaluations for all drills (*Success Goals*), and
- a complete test bank of written questions.

The series textbook, *Instructional Design for Teaching Physical Activities*, explains the *steps to success* model, which is the basis for the Steps to Success Activity Series. Teacher educators can use this text in their professional preparation classes to help future teachers and coaches learn how to design effective physical activity programs in school, recreation, or community teaching and coaching settings.

After identifying the need for participant, instructor, and teacher educator texts, we refined the *steps to success* instructional design model and developed prototypes for the participant's and the instructor's books. Once these prototypes were fine-tuned, we carefully selected authors for the activities who were not only thoroughly familiar with their sports but had years of experience in teaching them. Each author had to be known as a gifted instructor who understands the teaching of sport so thoroughly that he or she could readily apply the *steps to success* model.

Next, all of the participant's and instructor's manuscripts were carefully developed to meet the guidelines of the *steps to success* model. Then our production team, along with outstanding artists, created a highly visual, user-friendly series of books.

The result: The Steps to Success Activity Series is the premier sports instructional series available today. The participant's books are the best available for helping you to become a master player, the instructor's guides help you to become a master teacher, and the teacher educator's text prepares you to design your own programs.

This series would not have been possible without the contributions of the following:

- Dr. Joan Vickers, instructional design expert,
- Dr. Rainer Martens, Publisher,
- the staff of Human Kinetics Publishers, and
- the *many* students, teachers, coaches, consultants, teacher educators, specialists, and administrators who shared their ideas—and dreams.

Judy Patterson Wright
Series Editor

Preface

Teaching soccer requires knowledge of the rules, skills, and tactics used by individuals, small groups, and teams. Coaches and teachers who previously excelled as players may have acquired such knowledge through actual game experience. However, good players do not always become good teachers of the game. And conversely, many successful coaches were not outstanding players. Although extensive playing experience may provide a greater understanding of the game, such experience is not a prerequisite for teaching or coaching. Rather, successful teachers and coaches know how to teach the skills and strategies of soccer. This text, *Teaching Soccer: Steps to Success*, provides you with a step-by-step plan to teach beginning students these essential soccer skills and tactics.

As a teacher or coach you must convey your enthusiasm and knowledge of the game to students. You must clearly explain and demonstrate the skills and strategies of soccer. Once students understand how to execute a specific skill or strategy, you must improve their performance of that task with a series of drills or exercises. You must also evaluate student performance and provide appropriate feedback. *Teaching Soccer: Steps to Success* contains all the information you need to accomplish these objectives.

As with any project of this magnitude, many people contributed to this book's preparation and completion, too many to mention them all by name. However, I would like to sincerely thank several individuals for their help and support. Special thanks go to June Decker, developmental editor, for her patience and encouragement throughout the writing process, to Judy Patterson Wright, who got me started on the project, and to Rob King, who helped put the finishing touches on the book. My sincere appreciation also goes to Betty Datig at the University of Pittsburgh for her help in preparing the manuscript and illustrations for the artists to sketch from.

Very special thanks go to Gail Ann, the love of my life, for her help with the book and, more important, for her constant support and understanding. I also thank Grete, Kirsten, Nikki, and Olin for their seemingly endless enthusiasm. Finally, I extend my sincere gratitude to the many coaches and players with whom I've had the privilege of sharing thoughts and ideas.

I dedicate this book to the memory of my father, Francis Luxbacher, who taught me how to play and enjoy soccer, and to my mother, Mary Ann Luxbacher, for her constant love and support in everything I do.

Joseph A. Luxbacher

Implementing the Steps to Success Staircase

This book is meant to be flexible for not only your students' needs but for your needs as well. It is common to hear that students' perceptions of a task change as the task is learned. However, it is often forgotten that teachers' perceptions and actions also change (Goc-Karp & Zakrajsek, 1987; Housner & Griffey, 1985; Imwold & Hoffman, 1983; Vickers, 1990).

More experienced or master teachers tend to approach the teaching of activities in a similar manner. They are highly organized (e.g., they do not waste time when getting groups together or by using long explanations); they integrate information (from biomechanics, kinesiology, exercise physiology, motor learning, sport psychology, cognitive psychology, instructional design, etc.); and they relate basic skills into the larger game or performance context, succinctly explaining why the basic skills, concepts, and tactics are important within the game or performance setting. Then, usually within a few minutes, they place their students into gamelike practice situations that progress in steps that follow logical manipulations of factors such as

- the number of people used in tactical situations;
- the number of skills used in combination;
- the implementation of player movement, ball movement, or a combination of both;
- the restrictions of space or time allotted;
- the speed of performance required of players;
- the intensity and duration of the drill or exercise;
- the number of touches permitted players to receive, control, and pass the ball;
- the velocity or pace of a served ball;
- the variation of trajectory for tossed or served balls;
- the number and size of goals used in small-sided game situations; and
- the achievement required by success goals.

This book will show you how the basic soccer skills and selected physiological, psychological, and other pertinent knowledge are interrelated (see Appendix A for an overview). You can use this information not only to gain insights into the various interrelationships but also to define the subject matter for soccer. The following questions offer specific suggestions for implementing this knowledge base and help you evaluate and improve your teaching methods, which include class organization, drills, objectives, progressions, and evaluations.

1. Under what conditions do you teach?
   - How much space is available?
   - What type of equipment is available?
   - What is the average class size?
   - How much time is allotted per class session?
   - How many class sessions do you teach?
   - Do you have any teaching assistants?

2. What are your students' initial skill levels?
   - Look for the rating charts located in the beginning of most steps (chapters) to identify the criteria that distinguish between beginning and advanced skill levels.

3. What is the best order to teach soccer skills?
   - Follow the sequence of steps (chapters) used in this book.
   - See Appendix B.1 for suggestions on when to introduce, review, or continue practicing each step.
   - Based on your answers to the previous questions, use the form in Appendix B.2 to put into order the steps that you will be able to cover in the time available.

4. What objectives do you want your students to accomplish by the end of a lesson, unit, or course?

- For your technique or qualitative objectives, select from the Student Keys to Success (or see the Keys to Success Checklists in *Soccer: Steps to Success*) that are provided for all basic skills.
- For your performance or quantitative objectives, select from the Success Goals provided for each drill.
- For written questions on safety, rules, technique, tactics, and psychological aspects of soccer, select from the Test Bank of written questions.
- See the Sample Individual Program (Appendix C.1) for selected technique and performance objectives for a 16-week unit.
- For unit objectives, adjust your total number of selected objectives to fit your unit length (use the form in Appendix C.2).
- For organizing daily objectives, see the Sample Lesson Plan in Appendix D.1, and modify the basic lesson plan form in Appendix D.2 to best fit your needs.

5. How will you evaluate your students?

- Read the section "Evaluation Ideas."
- Decide on your type of grading system; you could use letter grades, pass-fail, satisfactory-unsatisfactory, percentages, point systems, plus-minus, levels of achievement (gold, silver, bronze), and so forth.

6. Which activities should be selected to achieve student objectives?

- Follow the drills for each step because they are specifically designed for large groups of students and are presented in a planned, easy-to-difficult order. Avoid a random approach to selecting drills.
- Modify drills as necessary to best fit each student's skill level by following the suggestions for decreasing and increasing the difficulty level of each drill.
- Ask your students to meet the Success Goal listed for each drill.
- Use the cross-reference to the corresponding step and drill in the participant's book, *Soccer: Steps to Success*, for class assignments or makeups. The bracketed notation [New Drill] after a drill title indicates that the drill appears only in this instructor's guide and will be new to your students.

7. What rules and expectations do you have for your class?

- For general management and safety guidelines, read the section "Preparing Your Class for Success."
- For specific guidelines, read the subhead "Group Management and Safety Tips" included with each drill.
- Let your students know what your rules are during your class orientation or first day of class. Then post the rules and discuss them often.

Teaching is a complex task, requiring you to make many decisions that affect both you and your students (see Figure 1). Use this book to create an effective and successful learning experience for you and everyone you teach. And remember, have fun too!

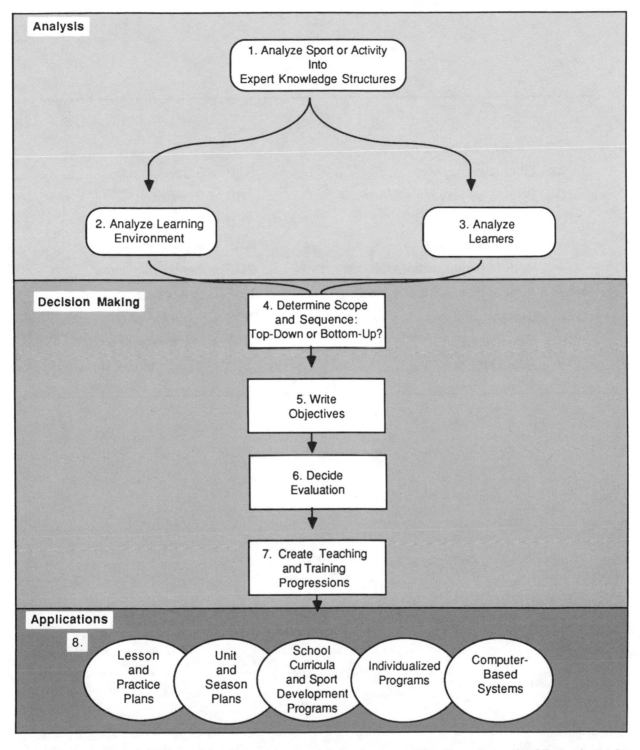

Figure 1. Instructional design model utilizing expert knowledge structures. *Note.* From *Instructional Design for Teaching Physical Activities* by J.N. Vickers (1990), Champaign, IL: Human Kinetics. Copyright 1990 by Joan N. Vickers. Reprinted by permission. This instructional design model has appeared in earlier forms in *Badminton: A Structures of Knowledge Approach* (p. 1) by J.N. Vickers and D. Brecht, 1987, Calgary, AB: University Printing Services, copyright 1987 by Joan N. Vickers; and "The Role of Expert Knowledge Structures in an Instructional Design Model for Physical Education" by J.N. Vickers, 1983, *Journal of Teaching in Physical Education*, **2**(3), p. 20, copyright 1983 by Joan N. Vickers. Adapted by permission.

Key

X = Offensive player

O = Defensive player

X⊛ = Player with the ball

– – → = Path of the ball

——→ = Path of player without the ball

〜〜〜→ = Path of player dribbling the ball

S = Server

GK = Goalkeeper

SW = Sweeper back

STB = Stopper back

RB = Right back

LB = Left back

RMF = Right midfielder

CMF = Center midfielder

LMF = Left midfielder

RFW = Right forward (winger)

LFW = Left forward (winger)

CS = Central striker (forward)

Preparing Your Class for Success

Successful teachers and coaches create an effective learning environment, one that is enjoyable, informative, and stimulating to students. Through the following principles of class management and organization you can create an optimal learning situation.

CLASS MANAGEMENT

Students must master a variety of skills in order to successfully play the game of soccer. Many of these skills may initially seem awkward and difficult to beginning students, because most are accustomed to using their hands and arms to throw or catch a ball. Students should also learn the tactics used by individuals, small groups, and teams in order to blend their talents into the efforts of the team as a whole. To foster optimal skill and tactical development, you must give considerable thought to the planning and organization of your class sessions.

Although soccer is traditionally an outdoor sport, all of the basic skills as well as individual and small group tactics can easily be taught indoors. Team tactics, due to the space requirements, are the only components of the game that may be difficult to teach indoors. If possible, teach students outdoors in a realistic soccer environment.

CLASS ORGANIZATION AND INSTRUCTIONAL TECHNIQUES

There is no substitute for preparation. Organize your class sessions to make maximum use of the time and space available. Each student should spend as much time on task as possible, and accomplishing that objective will require careful planning on your part. You should take into consideration the primary objectives of the lesson, available equipment and space requirements, the total number of students, and their overall levels of experience and ability. Use the following suggestions to help make the most efficient use of your contact time with students.

1. Teach yourself the basic soccer skills before trying to teach them to others. You should be able to demonstrate the various methods of passing and receiving the ball, heading, dribbling, shielding, tackling, and shooting. Modeling can be a very effective tool when supplemented with verbal instruction.

2. The more times a student can touch the ball in practice, the more quickly he or she will develop the skills required to play the game. Ideally, you should provide a soccer ball for each student. If that is not possible, have at least one ball for every two students. An ample supply of balls enables you to keep all students active throughout the entire lesson, and thus maximize time on task. Avoid situations requiring students to stand in long lines or be inactive for long periods.

3. Conduct a realistic lesson. Consider the ability of your students, then plan a practice that will challenge them to reach a higher level of performance. Try to incorporate the important elements of skill, fitness, and tactics into each drill or exercise. But remember not to make the drills so difficult that students experience only failure and frustration.

4. Focus each session on a central theme, for example, improving shooting skills. All drills and exercises then relate somehow to the theme. Don't try to cover too many different topics in a single lesson, particularly with beginning students. Let students progress one step at a time.

5. For each class session develop a rhythm that simulates the physical stress in an actual soccer match. Alternate high- and low-intensity drills and exercises.

6. Simplify your descriptions and explanations of drills and exercises. Briefly

introduce the topic and then get students involved.

7. Use a progressive sequence of drills. Each exercise should lay the foundation for the next. Progress to more complex drills as students experience success.

8. Make practice fun. Be innovative in designing your drills and exercises. Students will be motivated to learn and improve their game if they enjoy what they are doing.

9. Practice skills and tactics in small groups rather than full field scrimmages. Small group situations (one versus one, two versus two, three versus two, etc.) ensure that each player will touch the ball many times in a relatively short time.

10. Use playing grids. A grid is a restricted space where two or more players can practice skills and tactics. The sizes of grids may vary, depending on the number of players involved and the specific purpose of the drill. In general, 10-by-10-yard grids or 10-by-20-yard grids are appropriate for most individual skills and small-group tactics. The use of grids serves to simulate game conditions, where space and time are usually limited by opposing players.

11. Finish each class session with a game-like situation. It need not be a regulation 11 versus 11 game. In fact, small-sided or modified games (five versus five, six versus six) are more beneficial because players touch the ball more often. The primary emphasis should be the skills and tactics practiced during the lesson.

12. Use teaching aids. Cones or flags, miniature goals, scrimmage vests, and rebound nets can all be useful in class sessions. Whenever possible, position equipment and materials in their appropriate locations before students arrive.

CLASS WARM-UP

All students should warm up at the beginning of each class session to prepare their bodies for the more vigorous activity that follows. A thorough warm-up serves to alleviate next-day muscle soreness and helps prevent muscle pulls. The warm-up session should consist of activities that promote blood flow and elevate muscle temperature as well as exercises for flexibility and agility. The duration of the warm-up can vary depending on the students, the exercises, and the environment. A period of 10 to 20 minutes will usually suffice.

As teacher, you must include a warm-up in every class session. Start by having students increase their heart rates before stretching by participating in light aerobic activity, such as jogging while dribbling a ball. After increasing their heart rates and elevating their muscle temperatures, students may safely stretch the muscle groups used when playing or practicing soccer. Be sure students stretch the hamstring, quadricep, groin, calf, back, and neck muscles.

Familiarize students with the proper method of stretching. Emphasize static as opposed to ballistic (bouncing) stretching. Students should slowly deepen the stretch until they feel tension in the appropriate muscles, then hold that position for 15 to 30 seconds. After relaxing for a few seconds, students should repeat the stretch. You should organize and lead the stretching exercises for the first few class periods. Once students become familiar with the exercises, you can choose a couple of students each period to conduct the stretching portion of the warm-up.

The following exercises can be used in your class warm-up. You can also choose from the individual flexibility exercises found in *Soccer: Steps to Success* in "Preparing Your Body for Success." Don't attempt to use all of these exercises in a single session, however. In fact, varying the warm-up from period to period helps prevent boredom among students.

Small Group Exercises

1. *Swivel hips:* Partners stand back to back about 2 feet apart. One player holds a ball. On your command—"Begin"—both students rotate their shoulders left and exchange the ball between them while keeping their feet

stationary. Then partners immediately rotate in the opposite direction and again exchange the ball. The exercise continues until partners have exchanged the ball 30 times.

2. *Under and over:* Partners stand back to back about 2 feet apart with feet spread shoulder-width apart. One holds a ball. Both students bend forward at the waist, reach back between their legs, and exchange the ball. They immediately return to an upright position, reach upward and back over their heads, and again exchange the ball. Continue the exchange under and over until partners have exchanged the ball 30 times.

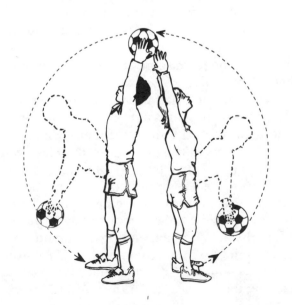

3. *Heading sit-ups:* Students pair up. One partner lies on the ground with knees bent while the other stands 5 yards from the partner's feet and tosses a ball toward him or her. The student on the ground sits up and heads the ball back to the server. Students repeat the exercise 20 times, then partners switch roles for 20 more heading sit-ups.

4. *Shadow dribbling:* Each student takes a ball and pairs with a partner, who also has a ball. One partner dribbles in random fashion within the field space while the other closely follows, dribbling as well. The leader can move anywhere within the playing area. The trailing player tries to imitate, or shadow, the movements of the leader. On your command —"Change"—students quickly turn and reverse roles. Continue the exercise for 5 minutes, with players constantly switching roles at your command.

5. *Juggling competition:* Organize students in groups of three with one ball per group, and position each group in a 10-by-10-yard grid. Instruct students to juggle the ball among themselves, using any body surface except the hands and arms to keep it airborne. Permit students only three touches of the ball before they pass it to another member of the group. Students are assessed 1 penalty point if they allow the ball to drop to the ground or kick the ball out of the grid. A player who totals 10 penalty points is eliminated from the game; eliminated players should practice individual juggling. Continue the exercise until only one player remains in each group, then reorganize groups and repeat the competition.

Large Group Exercises

1. *Soccer dodge ball:* Divide students into two equal teams. Position members of Team A within a 30-by-30-yard playing area. Position members of Team B, each with a ball, outside of the playing area. On your command—"Go!"—Team B players dribble into the area and attempt to pass their balls to hit players from Team A. Team A players are eliminated from the game if hit. A player must be hit below the knees to be eliminated. Players who are eliminated should leave the playing area and practice ball juggling together. The game continues until all Team A players have been eliminated. Teams then switch roles and repeat the drill. The team that eliminates its opponents in the shortest time wins. Play best two out of three games.

2. *Passing by the numbers:* Divide the class in groups of 8 to 12 students. Position each group in a 40-by-40-yard area. Instruct each player to call out a number, beginning with 1 and continuing up to the number of players in the group. Tell students to remember who has the number that is one higher than theirs. Three or four students in each group have balls. The exercise begins with all the students jogging (or dribbling) within the area. Each student with a ball locates the teammate numbered directly above him or her and passes to that person. The player with the highest number passes to Player 1 to complete the cycle. All students should move continuously throughout the exercise. Play for 5 to 10 minutes.

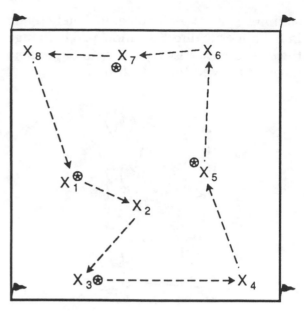

Sample passing cycle for "Passing by the numbers."

3. *Nutmeg races:* Divide the class into two equal teams. Position players from Team A evenly across a 20-by-20-yard area. Team A players must remain stationary with feet spread about 18 inches apart. Position players of Team B, each with a ball, outside of the playing area.

The game consists of two 5-minute halves. At your command—"Go!"—Team B players dribble into the playing area and pass the ball through the legs of (or "nutmeg") as many opponents as they can in 5 minutes. Players cannot nutmeg the same opponent twice in succession. Each player keeps track of how many nutmegs he or she accomplishes during the 5-minute half. Individual totals are combined for the team score at the end of the first half of play.

For the second half the teams switch roles. Compare team scores at the end of the game. The team with the most nutmegs wins.

4. *Chain tag:* All students in the class can participate in this exercise. Designate two students as "it" and position them outside the playing area. Position all remaining students within a playing area of about 30 by 30 yards. (Vary the area size depending on the number of students.) At your command—"Go!"—the students who are "it" enter the area to chase and tag the free players. When an "it" player tags a free player, they join hands to form a chain. The chains gradually increase in length

as more students are tagged. Only two chains are permitted; they cannot split into smaller chains. Continue the exercise until all free players have been tagged and are part of a chain. Designate two other students as "it" and repeat the exercise.

5. *Dribble freeze tag:* You can play this game with an unlimited number of students. Designate two students as "it" and position them outside the playing area. Position all remaining students, each with a ball, inside a playing area of about 25 by 25 yards. (Vary the area size depending upon the number of students.)

On your command—"Go!"—students within the area begin random dribbling. After 30 seconds the students who are "it" enter the area and try to tag the dribbling students. A dribbler who is tagged is "frozen" and must sit on his or her ball. Free dribblers can release the frozen players by tagging them. Continue the game for 3 minutes or until all dribblers are frozen, whichever comes first. Designate two other students as "it" and repeat the game.

6. *Speed dribbling:* Play this drill with an unlimited number of students. Divide the class into two equal teams. Mark off parallel start and finish lines about 30 yards apart. Position all students, each with a ball, 2 to 3 yards apart along the starting line. On your command—"Go!"—students dribble at maximum speed to the finish line, turn, and dribble back to the starting line. The team whose players all return their balls to the starting line first is awarded 1 point. Repeat the race after a brief rest. The first team to total 5 points wins.

7. *Side shuffle game:* Divide the class into three equal teams. Line up the teams side by side (about 3 yards between lines) in single-file columns facing you. Number the columns 1, 2, and 3. To begin the exercise call out one of the column numbers. If you call out "Column 1," Columns 1 and 2 change places using a sideways shuffle. If you call you "Column 2," Columns 2 and 3 change places. If you call out "Column 3," Columns 1 and 3 change places. Issue commands randomly so students cannot anticipate your call. Remind students that after changing positions they assume the number of the column space to which they moved. Any student who moves in the wrong direction is penalized 1 point. Play the game for 3 minutes. The team with the fewest penalty points at the end of the exercise wins. Repeat several times.

8. *Foxes and rabbits:* Divide the class into two equal teams. Assign a name to each team. (Here I will use the names Kickers and Strikers.) Students position, each with a soccer ball, in a 30-by-30-yard area. Use cones or flags to designate two 5-by-5-yard safety zones in opposite corners of the playing area.

On your command—"Go!"—all students dribble in random fashion within the area, staying out of the safety zones. Let students dribble for about 60 seconds, then shout one of the team names, for example, "Strikers!" Then the Strikers quickly dribble into either safety zone while the Kickers leave their balls to tag Striker players before they reach a safety zone. The students who chase are "foxes" while the players who dribble are "rabbits." Rabbits are protected once they enter either safety zone. Award the Strikers 1 point for each player who reaches a safety zone before being tagged. Repeat the exercise with teams alternating as foxes and rabbits. End the game after teams have had equal opportunity to be rabbits. The team totaling the most points wins.

CLASS COOL-DOWN EXERCISES

All students must participate in a brief cool-down at the end of the practice session. The cool-down brings body functions back near normal and stretches the major muscle groups used during the class session. A cool-down also provides time to summarize the most important points of the lesson. The stretching exercises that students used during warm-up can also be used during cool-down. You can refer to "Preparing Your Body for Success" in *Soccer: Steps to Success* for additional exercises.

EQUIPMENT

A variety of equipment and teaching aids can help you create the most effective learning situation. Equipment needs will depend upon the class size and available space. If your budget permits, consider purchasing the following equipment and coaching aids.

1. The soccer ball is obviously the most important item of equipment. Try to

provide one ball per student. An ample supply of balls enables you to keep all students active at the same time and increases your drill and exercise options.

The official adult ball (Size #5) is 27 to 28 inches in circumference and weighs 14 to 16 ounces. Hand-sewn leather balls are the best choice but are also fairly expensive. Inexpensive synthetic-leather soccer balls should be adequate for your class. Do not use rubber soccer balls, which do not impact off the foot with sufficient velocity and tend to hurt players' feet.

When conducting your class indoors, consider using special indoor balls that are very soft and cannot be kicked as hard. These are especially effective for teaching skills to beginning students. Whenever possible, however, use regulation Size #5 balls.

2. Use small cones and flags to mark off grid areas, represent goalposts, construct dribbling circuits, and designate other drill areas.

3. Use regulation-sized goals for shooting drills and practicing goalkeeping skills. Use minigoals for small-sided (fewer-player) games and indoor classes.

4. Use scrimmage vests to differentiate attackers from defenders in small-group situations or one team from another in actual games. Vests come in a variety of colors and are relatively inexpensive.

5. All students should wear shin guards to safeguard against injury. A variety of models are available. Most fit snugly against the shin, weigh only a few ounces, and are relatively inexpensive.

6. Goalkeepers should wear proper equipment. Padded goalkeeper pants and long-sleeved jerseys with padded elbows will help prevent serious bumps and bruises that can occur when a goalie dives to make a save.

7. A diving pit filled with sawdust or sand provides a soft surface for goalkeepers to practice diving skills.

8. A pendulum ball attached to a rope and hung from a horizontal bar can help with practicing heading and passing techniques. The height of the ball should be adjusted to suit the type of skill (heading, volley passing, etc.) being practiced.

9. A magnetic board with movable players is an excellent visual aid for explaining tactics or systems of play to your students.

10. By using a kickwall as a target or rebounding surface, students can practice all basic passing, receiving, and shooting skills.

11. If you use audiovisual equipment to film students during practices and games they can observe themselves as you point out both positive and negative aspects of performance.

SAFETY

Because soccer is a contact sport, a certain amount of physical risk accompanies participation in drills or games. Accidental collisions, twisted ankles and knees, and bruised shins sometimes do result. As teacher you must make the classroom environment as safe as possible. Even though you won't be able to prevent all injuries, you can implement measures to keep them to a minimum.

You must start by establishing guidelines for appropriate behavior. A general set of class rules and regulations will make the practice and playing environment as safe as possible. You should also establish a standard procedure to deal with any injuries that occur. Ask players to inform you of any injuries, however minor, so you can maintain accurate records. Familiarize all students with the injury procedure at the beginning of the school term or playing season.

The following guidelines, coupled with common sense, will help you structure a safe learning environment for your students.

1. When conducting class outdoors, clear the playing surface of any sharp objects, such as glass or metal.

2. When conducting class indoors, make sure the floor is free of loose dirt and dust. A dirty floor is often very slippery and may result in student injuries.

3. Store any unused soccer balls a safe distance from the practice area so that students do not accidentally step on a ball.

4. Emphasize good body control at all times during drills/exercises and games. Instruct students to play the ball, not the opponent. Also, forbid field players to contact a goalkeeper who has possession of the ball.

5. Establish a set of verbal signals and make sure all students become familiar with the terminology.

6. Do not permit mischief (wrestling, throwing balls, etc.) during class breaks.

7. Always allow a few yards between drill or game areas so that players from adjacent groups do not inadvertently collide. *Never* organize drills so that two grids share a boundary line.

8. Organize drills to keep all students in view.

9. Require all students to wear suitable gym shoes indoors or soccer shoes outdoors. Do not permit students to practice in bare feet or socks.

10. Do not let students wear watches, chains, earrings, or other jewelry, which may endanger them or others.

11. Do not allow students to chew gum while practicing or playing in a game.

12. Prohibit hanging on the goalposts or crossbar. Also, be sure the goalposts are securely fastened to the ground so that they cannot fall over on a student.

PRECLASS CHECKLIST

Preparation is a key to successful teaching. Planning can save valuable practice time during class and make the class flow more smoothly. Organize drills in a progression from basic to complex, with initial exercises laying the foundation for those that follow. Structure the lesson for as much time on task as possible.

The following checklist provides a list of preclass duties for preparing each lesson.

1. Make sure all balls are properly inflated.
2. Have alternative activities planned in the event of poor weather or absenteeism due to illness or injury.

3. Position equipment (cones, flags, etc.) prior to students' arrival for class.

4. Post preclass warm-up exercises for students who arrive early.

5. Provide water or sport drinks during breaks in practice, particularly on hot and humid days.

6. Post emergency phone numbers (ambulance, hospital, etc.) conspicuously.

NINE LEGAL DUTIES

As teacher, you have certain legal responsibilities to your students. Failure to fulfill these duties may constitute negligence on your part and have serious legal consequences. Familiarize yourself with the following legal duties and adequately fulfill each when teaching your soccer class.

1. Adequate Supervision

Physically organize your class so that all students are in view at all times. In addition, never leave the class doing drills unsupervised for any length of time. If you must leave the gym or field, stop the exercises and instruct the students to rest until you return.

2. Sound Planning

Use drills and exercises appropriate for the age and ability of your students. Order drills in a progression from basic to complex and center them around a theme or objective.

3. Inherent Risks

Advise students that certain inherent risks accompany participation in soccer. Students can minimize risks by using correct skill execution, maintaining adequate physical fitness, and playing in a controlled manner.

4. Safe Learning Environment

Provide a safe environment for practice and games. Refer to the information under "Safety" earlier in this chapter for suggestions on making the playing environment as safe as possible.

5. Evaluating Students' Physical Status for Participation

Assess the physical capabilities of your students and plan your classes accordingly. Because soccer requires a high degree of aerobic and anaerobic fitness, constantly watch for signs of fatigue in your students. The likelihood of injury increases as students become tired. Check for any injuries that could limit performance in drills or exercises.

The drills and exercises in this book are appropriate for high school and college students and many can also be used with younger players. However, because each teaching situation is unique, use good judgment in selecting drills for your specific group of students.

6. Matching Students

Fairly match or equate students in drills and competitive situations. Failure to do so can result in a dangerous situation for which you are liable. For example, pairing a large, advanced player with a small, inexperienced partner in a block tackle drill puts the smaller player at undue risk of injury. Assess the age, ability, size, and strength of your students and match them accordingly.

7. Emergency First Aid Procedures

Become familiar with the emergency first aid procedures of the school or institution your program is associated with. Provide proper first aid and plan emergency medical procedures that can be put into immediate action. Post emergency medical phone numbers by the phone nearest your classroom or field. Such preparation could save precious moments in a time of crisis. If injuries do occur, keep accurate records of the who, what, where, when, why, and how of the incident.

8. Other Legal Concerns

Assure that the basic civil rights of your students are not violated in your class.

9. General Legal Concerns

Though you may take every possible precaution, accidents sometimes occur. Consider carrying personal liability insurance to protect yourself in case of a lawsuit. As mentioned earlier, you must keep detailed records of all injuries that occur during class participation.

Step 1 Passing and Receiving Ground Balls

Teamwork is essential for successful soccer. Combination play cannot occur, however, until students master the skills used to pass and receive the ball. These skills provide the foundation for all other techniques and tactics used in game play. Therefore, emphasize the development of proper passing and receiving skills early in the learning process.

Passing depends on accuracy, correct pace, and timing of the release. Also, students must be able to pass the ball along the ground whenever possible: Ground passes are more easily received and controlled than lofted passes. Receivers should always attempt to cushion the impact, control the ball within range of their feet, and then protect the ball from a challenging opponent. Whether passing or receiving the ball, students should execute the skill in a smooth, fluid manner.

Inside of Foot Pass Rating

BEGINNING LEVEL	ADVANCED LEVEL
Preparation • Shoulders at an angle to target • Balance foot behind ball • Balance leg straight and stiff • Vision focused on field or opponent	• Shoulders square to target • Balance foot planted beside ball • Balance leg slightly flexed • Head steady with vision focused on ball
Execution • Body behind ball • Kicking foot loose or uncertain • Ball contacted near toes • Ball contacted above or below its horizontal midline • Vision focused on field or opponent rather than on ball	• Body over ball • Kicking foot firmly positioned • Ball contacted with inside surface of foot midway between heel and toes • Ball contacted in center by inside of kicking foot • Head steady with vision focused on ball
Follow-Through • Momentum slows at point of contact • Weak follow-through • Shoulders at an angle to target • Player fails to move into open space after passing	• Momentum forward through point of contact • Sufficient follow-through • Shoulders remain square to target • Player moves forward into open space after passing

Outside of Foot Pass Rating

BEGINNING LEVEL	ADVANCED LEVEL
Preparation	
• Balance foot planted ahead of ball	• Balance foot placed slightly behind and to side of ball
• Balance leg straight and stiff	• Balance leg flexed and relaxed
• Kicking foot slightly or fully flexed	• Kicking foot fully extended and angled inward
• Vision focused on field or opponent	• Head steady with vision focused on ball
Execution	
• Arms tight against sides	• Arms extended out to sides for balance
• Kicking foot uncertain during contact	• Kicking foot firmly positioned during contact
• Player contacts ball with partial outer edge of instep	• Ball contacted on full outer portion of instep
• Foot contacts near outer edge of ball	• Ball contacted just inside its vertical midline
• Vision focused on field or opponent rather than on ball	• Head steady with vision focused on ball
Follow-Through	
• Weight remains back	• Weight transfers forward through point of contact
• Kicking motion of leg is straight or follows an outside-in arc	• Kicking motion follows an inside-out arc
• Weak follow-through	• Follow-through to waist level or higher
• Player fails to move into open space after passing	• Player moves into open space after passing

Instep Pass Rating

BEGINNING LEVEL	ADVANCED LEVEL
Preparation	
• Player approaches from directly behind ball	• Player approaches ball from a slight angle
• Balance foot placed behind ball	• Balance foot planted beside ball
• Balance leg straight and stiff	• Balance leg flexed at knee
• Knee of kicking leg is behind ball	• Knee of kicking leg is over ball
• Kicking foot slightly or fully flexed rather than fully extended	• Kicking foot fully extended
• Arms next to body and balance poor	• Arms extended out to side for balance
• Vision focused on field or opponent rather than on ball	• Vision focused on ball

(Cont.)

BEGINNING LEVEL	ADVANCED LEVEL
Execution	
• Weight remains back on contact	• Weight moves forward
• Kicking motion weak	• Powerful snap of kicking leg
• Ball contacted on part of instep near toes	• Ball contacted on full instep
• Kicking foot wobbly or uncertain at contact	• Kicking foot extended and firmly positioned
Follow-Through	
• Momentum slows at point of contact	• Momentum moves forward through point of contact
• Weak follow-through	• Complete follow-through to waist level or higher
• Player fails to move into open space after passing ball	• Player moves into open space after passing ball

Error Detection and Correction for Ground Passes

Passing errors destroy the teamwork vital to maintaining possession of the ball and scoring goals. However, beginning players often experience initial difficulty in accurately passing the ball, particularly when pressed by opponents. Most errors occur due to one or more of the following:

1. Incorrect position of the balance foot
2. Failure to firmly position the kicking foot
3. Improper kicking technique
4. Insufficient follow-through of the kicking leg

As you observe students, focus your attention on these common performance errors.

ERROR

CORRECTION

Inside of the Foot Pass

1. The ball travels up into the air.

2. The ball does not travel to the intended target.

1. Have the student contact the ball directly through its horizontal midline with the inside surface of the kicking foot.

2. Tell the player to square shoulders with the intended target, place the balance foot beside the ball, and point it toward the target. Make sure the kicking foot remains firm as it contacts the ball.

ERROR 🚫   **CORRECTION**

3. The pass lacks sufficient pace.

3. Tell the student to allow a greater follow-through of the kicking leg.

Outside of the Foot Pass

1. The ball travels up into the air.

1. Tell the student to lean slightly forward when contacting the ball. The kicking foot should be firmly positioned, extended downward and inward. The ball should be contacted on the outside portion of the instep.

2. The pass lacks accuracy.

2. Tell the student to contact the ball with as much foot surface area as possible. The student's head should be held steady with vision focused on the ball.

3. Too much spin is imparted to the ball.

3. Have the student contact the ball only slightly off center, to the left or right of its vertical midline. If the ball is contacted too close to its outer edge too much spin will occur.

Instep Pass

1. The ball travels up into the air.

1. Tell the student not to lean back when kicking. Emphasize that the balance foot should be planted beside the ball and the knee of the kicking leg and the whole body should be over the ball at the moment of contact.

2. The pass lacks accuracy.

2. Have the student square shoulders with the target and keep the kicking foot firmly positioned as it contacts the ball.

3. The ball curves to either the left or right of the target.

3. The student has failed to square shoulders with the target or has improperly positioned the kicking foot. Tell the student to square shoulders with the target and contact the center of the ball with the full instep surface of the foot.

Receiving With Inside of Foot Rating

BEGINNING LEVEL	ADVANCED LEVEL
Preparation	
• Body positioned to left or right of oncoming ball	• Player positions in line with oncoming ball
• Player waits for ball to arrive	• Player moves forward to meet oncoming ball
• Player fails to reach out with receiving foot	• Receiving leg and foot extend to meet oncoming ball
• Receiving foot not firmly positioned	• Receiving foot firmly positioned before it contacts ball
• Receiving foot points toward ball rather than sideways	• Receiving foot positioned sideways to ball
• Vision focused on field or opponent rather than on ball	• Head steady with vision focused on ball
Execution	
• Ball rolls under player's foot	• Inside surface of receiving foot contacts center of ball
• Ball bounces away from receiving foot	• Player cushions impact by withdrawing receiving foot as ball contacts
• Player receives ball in space where opponent is positioned	• Ball is controlled and directed away from opponent
Follow-Through	
• Player stops ball completely	• Ball is guided in direction of player's next movement
• Head is down and vision on ball	• Head is up with vision on field

Receiving With Outside of Foot Rating

BEGINNING LEVEL	ADVANCED LEVEL
Preparation	
• Player positions with ball between him or her and opponent	• Body positioned sideways between ball and opponent
• Receiving foot flexed or rotated outward	• Receiving foot extended down and rotated inward
• Receiving foot wobbly	• Receiving foot firmly positioned
• Player fails to reach out with foot to meet ball	• Receiving foot reaches out to meet ball
• Vision focused on field or opponent rather than on ball	• Head is steady with vision focused on ball

(Cont.)

Receiving With Outside of Foot Rating (Continued)

BEGINNING LEVEL	ADVANCED LEVEL
Execution • Ball bounces away out of control • Player leaves ball open to opponent • Player stops ball completely • Player receives ball in space occupied by opponent	• Receiving foot and leg withdraw to cushion impact as ball arrives • Body positioned sideways between the ball and opponent • Player controls ball but does not stop it completely • Player pushes ball into space away from opponent
Follow-Through • Player remains stationary with ball • Head down with vision on ball instead of on field	• Player pushes ball in direction of next movement • Head up with vision on surrounding field

Error Detection and Correction for Receiving Ground Balls

Receiving and controlling ground balls is relatively easy to learn. As you observe students, make sure they align their bodies with the oncoming ball, focus their vision on it, and cushion the impact as the ball arrives. Failure to perform one or more of these acts will usually result in performance errors.

ERROR   **CORRECTION**

Receiving With the Inside of the Foot

1. The ball rolls over the player's foot and out of range of control.

2. The ball bounces off the foot and out of control.

1. Have the player contact the horizontal center of the ball with the inside surface of the foot. If contacted too near the ground, the ball will roll over the foot.

2. Tell the student to withdraw the receiving foot to cushion the impact as the ball arrives.

ERROR    **CORRECTION**

3. The ball rolls under the student's foot.	3. Tell the student to focus vision on the ball as it arrives. The inside surface of the foot should contact the horizontal midline of the ball.

Receiving With the Outside of the Foot

1. The ball bounces out of range of control.	1. The student should withdraw the receiving foot to cushion the impact as the ball arrives.
2. The student fails to protect the ball from a challenging opponent.	2. Have the student position sideways between the opponent and the ball. The foot farthest from the opponent should control the ball.

Ground Ball Passing and Receiving Drills

1. Off the Wall
[Corresponds to *Soccer*, Step 1, Drill 1]

Group Management and Safety Tips
- Students should stand at least 3 yards apart as they pass and receive the ball off a wall.
- Students should watch out for other classmates when retrieving a stray ball.

Equipment
- 1 ball per student

Instructions to Class
- ''Position yourself with a ball about 5 yards from the gym wall.''
- ''Use the inside of your foot to pass the ball off the wall so that it rebounds to you.''
- ''Receive and control each rebound with the inside of your foot.''
- ''Try to use only two touches to receive and pass the ball. Control the ball with your first touch as it rebounds, then use your second touch to pass the ball off the wall again.''
- ''Pass the ball off the wall 20 times with each foot.''

Student Option
- ''You may alternate your passing with left and right foot or pass and receive 20 times with the right foot, then 20 with the left.''

Student Keys to Success

Passing
- Firmly position passing foot.
- Strike the ball through its center.
- Use smooth follow-through.
- Focus vision on the ball.

Receiving

- Firmly position receiving foot.
- Withdraw receiving foot at ball contact.
- Prepare ball with first touch, and pass ball with second touch.
- Receive and prepare to pass the ball in one fluid motion.

Student Success Goal

- 35 two-touch passes off the wall out of 40 attempts

To Decrease Difficulty

- Move closer to the wall.
- Take more time between passes.
- Decrease the Success Goal.

To Increase Difficulty

- Move farther from the wall.
- Speed up repetitions.
- Increase the Success Goal.

2. Partner Pass

[Corresponds to *Soccer*, Step 1, Drill 2]

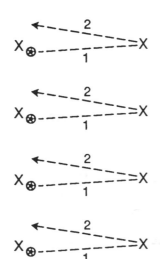

Group Management and Safety Tips

- Position groups at least 3 yards apart.
- Instruct students to pass the ball at their own pace. If the class has obvious deficiencies in passing skills tell students to pass the balls simultaneously at your command.

Equipment

- 1 ball per student pair

Instructions to Class

- "Choose a partner and stand about 5 yards apart, facing one another."
- "Use the inside of your foot to pass the ball back and forth with your partner."
- "Use only two touches to pass and receive the ball. Control and prepare the ball with the first touch, and return the ball to your partner with the second."

- "Alternate the passing foot."
- "Pass the ball so your partner need move no more than one step to receive it. Concentrate on accuracy and correct pace of your passes."
- "Each of you pass the ball 25 times with each foot."

Student Option

- "Receive the ball with whichever foot is closer to it. You needn't alternate feet each time you receive the ball."

Student Keys to Success

Passing

- Keep passing foot firm.
- Focus vision on the ball.
- Strike the ball directly through its center.
- Follow through smoothly.

Receiving

- Move to meet the ball.
- Withdraw the receiving foot at contact.
- Prepare the ball with the first touch, and pass it with the second.

Student Success Goal

- 50 two-touch errorless passes with your partner

To Decrease Difficulty

- Reduce the distance between partners.
- Slow down repetitions.
- Decrease the Success Goal.

To Increase Difficulty

- Increase the distance between partners.
- Speed up repetitions.

3. *Partner to Partner*
[Corresponds to *Soccer*, Step 1, Drill 4]

Group Management and Safety Tips

- Position student groups several yards apart.
- Caution students to avoid colliding with classmates when chasing errant passes.

Equipment

- 1 ball per student pair

Instructions to Class

- "Choose a partner and stand 25 yards apart, facing one another."
- "Pass the ball along the ground to your partner. He or she receives and controls the ball and then passes it back to you."
- "Your partner should not have to move more than 2 yards to receive your pass."
- "Alternate your feet and use only two touches to pass and receive the ball."
- "Execute 40 passes each."

Student Options

- "Practice both the instep and outside-of-the-foot techniques for passing and receiving."

- "Match the distance between yourselves to your ability and the type of pass being used."

Student Keys to Success

Passing

- Focus vision on the ball.
- Firmly position the kicking foot as it contacts the ball.
- Follow through completely.

Receiving

- Move to meet the ball.
- Withdraw the receiving foot at contact.
- Control the ball with the first touch.

Student Success Goals

- 34 of 40 balls accurately passed to partner
- 34 of 40 balls received, controlled, and returned using only two touches

To Decrease Difficulty

- Move partners closer.

- Permit three or four touches to receive and pass the ball.
- Permit student to move 4 yards to receive a pass.

To Increase Difficulty

- Increase the distance between partners.

- Strictly limit students to two touches to receive and pass a ball.
- Permit players to move only 1 yard to receive the ball.

4. Receive, Pass and Change Lines

[Corresponds to *Soccer*, Step 1, Drill 5]

Group Management and Safety Tips

- Make lines of only two or three players: Longer lines waste learning time by making students stand and wait for a turn.
- Instruct students to avoid colliding with classmates when changing lines.

Equipment

- 1 ball per two groups of students

Instructions to Class

- "Divide into groups of two or three."
- "Line up your group single file facing another single-file group. Leave about 10 yards between groups."
- "The first player in one line has a ball and begins the drill by passing to the first person in the opposite line and then sprinting to the end of that line."
- "The player in the opposite line receives, controls, and returns the ball to the first person in the other line, and then sprints to the end of that line."
- "Continue until each player has passed and received 30 balls. Use only two touches to receive and pass the ball."

Student Option

- "Practice with both the inside and outside of the foot to pass and receive the ball."

Student Keys to Success

- Keep all passes on the ground.
- Focus on accuracy and correct pace of passes.

Student Success Goals

- 28 of 30 balls accurately passed to classmate
- 28 of 30 balls received and returned using only two touches

To Decrease Difficulty

- Move lines closer.
- Permit players three or four touches to control and pass the ball.
- Permit the drill at half speed.

To Increase Difficulty

- Move lines farther apart.
- Strictly limit students to two touches to receive and pass.
- Perform the drill at game speed.

5. *Monkey in the Middle*

[Corresponds to *Soccer*, Step 1, Drill 6]

Group Management and Safety Tips

- Maintain at least 5 yards between groups.
- Allow students to self-pace the drill to promote successful execution. Instruct students to increase the speed of repetition as they become more confident.

Equipment

- 2 balls for every group of 3 students

Instructions to Class

- "Divide into groups of three."
- "Two students per group take a ball and stand 20 yards apart to act as servers. The third person positions midway between the servers."
- "The servers alternate passing their balls to the central player, who receives, controls, and returns each pass to the server. After each return the central player quickly turns to receive a pass from the opposite server."
- "Continue the drill until the central player has received and returned 20 balls. Then switch places and repeat the exercise."
- "Try to receive and return each pass using only two touches."

Student Options

- "Practice both the inside- and outside-of-the-foot technique to pass."
- "Practice both the inside- and outside-of-the-foot technique to receive and control the ball."

Student Keys to Success

- Focus on accuracy and correct pace of passes.
- Central player should move to meet the ball.
- Cushion the ball impact when controlling it.

Student Success Goal

- 18 of 20 balls received and returned from the central position using only two touches

To Decrease Difficulty

- Move players closer.
- Perform drill at half speed.
- Permit three or four touches to receive, control, and return ball.

To Increase Difficulty

- Move players farther apart.
- Perform drill at game speed.
- Strictly limit students to two touches to receive, control, and return the ball.

6. *Pass and Receive With a Moving Target*

[Corresponds to *Soccer*, Step 1, Drill 8]

Group Management and Safety Tip

- Caution students to watch out for other classmates as they move about.

Equipment

- 1 ball per group of 3 players

Instructions to Class

- "Divide into groups of three. One student per group has a ball. The other two students position at least 25 yards from the person with the ball."

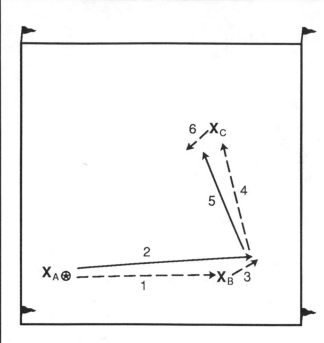

- "On my command, jog (or dribble) in random fashion."
- "The student with the ball passes it to another group member, then sprints to a position near the player who received the ball. The receiver passes back to the first player, who controls the return pass, passes the ball to the third group member, and sprints to a position near that player."
- "Try to use only two touches to control and pass the ball."

- "Remain in constant motion. All passes must be 25 yards or greater."
- "Continue the drill until the player who started with the ball executes 20 passes. Then switch roles and repeat."

Student Option

- "Use either the instep or outside of the foot to pass and receive the ball."

Student Keys to Success

- Serve the ball so that players can receive it without breaking stride.
- Strive for accuracy and correct pace of passes.

Student Success Goals

- 16 of 20 balls received and controlled using only two touches
- 16 of 20 balls accurately passed to classmates

To Decrease Difficulty

- Move players closer.
- Permit three or four touches to receive and control the ball.
- Perform the drill at half speed.

To Increase Difficulty

- Move players farther apart.
- Strictly limit players to two touches to receive and control the ball.
- Perform the drill at game speed.

7. Circle Drill
[Corresponds to *Soccer*, Step 1, Drill 9]

Group Management and Safety Tips

- Position groups at least 5 yards apart.
- Use tape or chalk indoors to outline circles 25 to 30 yards in diameter. Use lime or appropriate field markers outdoors.

Equipment

- 1 ball per group of 4 students
- Tape, chalk, or markers to outline a circle for each group

Instructions to Class

- "Divide into groups of four. Within each group number yourselves 1, 2, 3, and 4 and position around the edge of a circle with a diameter of 25 to 30 yards. Player 1 has a ball."
- "The player with the ball passes it to the student numbered above him or her (1 to 2, 2 to 3, etc.)."

- "After passing the ball the player immediately sprints to the position on the circle where the ball was passed."
- "The player who received the ball passes it to the player numbered above him or her and sprints to that position."
- "Player 4 passes to Player 1 to complete the cycle."
- "Try to use only two touches to receive and pass the ball."
- "Continue until each player has passed and received 40 balls."

Student Option

- "Pass and receive ball using either the outside of the foot or the instep."

Student Keys to Success

- Focus on pass accuracy.
- Receive and pass the ball with two touches.

Student Success Goal

- 35 of 40 balls received and passed using only two touches

To Decrease Difficulty

- Perform drill at half speed.
- Permit three or four touches to receive and pass the ball.
- Allow players to remain in place on the circle after each pass.
- Make the circle smaller.

To Increase Difficulty

- Perform drill at game speed.
- Make the circle larger.
- Strictly limit students to two touches to receive and pass the ball.

8. Keep-Away
[Corresponds to *Soccer*, Step 1, Drill 10]

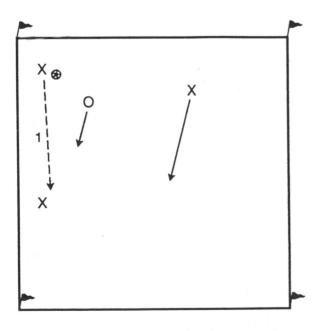

Group Management and Safety Tips

- Use cones, flags, or chalk to mark off a series of 10-by-10-yard areas prior to student arrival.
- Position grids at least 5 yards apart so that students from adjacent areas do not accidentally collide.
- Prohibit slide tackling.

Equipment

- 1 ball per group of 4 students
- Cones, flags, or chalk to mark off the grids
- Scrimmage vests for attackers

Instructions to Class

- "Divide into groups of four."
- "Choose one group member to play defender, and designate the remaining players as attackers. Position yourselves within a 10-by-10-yard area."
- "The three attackers try to keep the ball from the defender while remaining in the grid area."

- "The attacking players receive 1 point for making 10 consecutive passes without the defender stealing the ball. If the ball goes out of the grid area, or is stolen by the defender, the attackers must start numbering consecutive passes again with 1."
- "Play for 5 minutes, then choose a different defender. I will signal the beginning and end of the drill."

Student Option

- "Use any appropriate passing and receiving techniques."

Students Keys to Success

Attackers

- Focus on accurate passing and receiving.
- Move to open space with and without the ball.
- Utilize entire grid area.
- Constantly change ball position to unbalance the defender.

Defender

- Maintain balance and control.
- Pressure the player with the ball.
- Anticipate the movements and passes of the attackers.

Student Success Goal

- Score at least 5 points in a 5 minute game.

To Decrease Difficulty for Attackers

- Make the area larger.
- Allow four attackers.
- Allow the attackers an unlimited number of touches when passing and receiving.

To Increase Difficulty for Attackers

- Make the area smaller.
- Limit the number of touches allowed the attackers when passing and receiving.

9. *Pass and Receive to Score*
[New Drill]

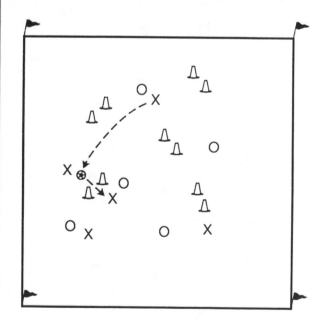

Group Management and Safety Tips

- Use cones, flags, or similar markers to outline a 40-by-40-yard area for each game. Use cones to designate five small goals, each 2 yards wide, at random positions in the playing area.
- Organize students into teams of four to six.

Equipment

- 1 ball per game
- Cones, flags, or similar markers to outline the playing fields and small goals
- Colored scrimmage vests to differentiate teams

Instructions to Class

- "Divide into two teams and position yourselves in a playing field. One team begins with the ball."

- "The team with the ball kicks off from the center of the playing area. Either team can score in any of the five goals and must defend all five goals when the opposing team has the ball. Players score 1 point by kicking the ball through a goal to a teammate on the other side. Points may be scored from either side of a goal, but consecutive scores through the same goal are not permitted."
- "An out-of-play ball is returned by a throw-in."
- "Play the game for 20 minutes with no pauses. The team that scores the most points wins."

Student Option

- None

Student Keys to Success

- Direct attacks toward less-guarded goals.
- Frequently change the point of attack.

Team Success Goal

- Score more points than the opposing team.

To Decrease Difficulty

- Increase goal size.
- Use more goals.

To Increase Difficulty

- Reduce the size of the playing area to require more control.
- Decrease goal size.

Step 2   Passing and Receiving Lofted Balls

Although most often students should play the ball along the ground, they should also learn to effectively pass and receive lofted balls. In some game situations a lofted, or chipped, pass is actually the better choice. For example, if an opposing player blocks the passing lane between two offensive teammates, one attacker can chip the ball over the opponent to the other attacker. Teach your students the techniques for both short- and long-chip passes.

Because the ball frequently leaves the ground during a soccer match in corner kicks, goal kicks, defensive clearances, crosses, and so forth, students must learn to receive and control a ball dropping out of the air. Students may use one of four body surfaces to receive balls out of the air: the instep, thigh, chest, or head. Students should learn to use each of these surfaces confidently. Teach students to choose the appropriate body surface before the ball's arrival. They must also align their body with the oncoming ball, then cushion the impact by withdrawing the body surface as the ball arrives.

Short Chip Pass Rating

BEGINNING LEVEL	ADVANCED LEVEL
Preparation • Balance foot placed behind ball • Balance leg stiff and straight • Kicking foot not fully extended • Vision focused on field or opponent rather than on ball	**Preparation** • Balance foot beside ball • Balance leg slightly flexed • Kicking foot fully extended • Head steady and vision focused on ball
Execution • Knee of kicking leg behind ball • Leans backward • Shoulders at an angle to target • Kicking foot wobbly • Weak snap of kicking leg • Foot contacts ball just below horizontal midline	**Execution** • Knee of kicking leg over ball • Leans slightly forward • Shoulders square with intended target • Kicking foot firmly positioned • Short, powerful leg snap • Instep of kicking foot wedged beneath ball
Follow-Through • Momentum stops at point of contact • Kicking leg sweeps slowly	**Follow-Through** • Momentum forward through point of contact • Minimal follow-through

Long Chip Pass Rating

BEGINNING LEVEL	ADVANCED LEVEL
Preparation • Balance foot directly beside ball • Balance leg stiff and straight • Kicking leg drawn back with foot somewhat flexed • Arms tight to sides • Vision focused on field or opponent rather than on ball	• Balance foot behind and to side of ball • Balance leg slightly flexed • Kicking leg drawn back with foot fully extended • Arms out to sides for balance • Head steady with vision focused on ball
Execution • Knee of kicking leg over ball • Shoulders at an angle to target • Kicking foot wobbly • Instep of foot contacts center of ball	• Knee of kicking leg slightly behind ball • Shoulders square with target • Kicking foot firmly positioned • Instep of foot driven through lower half of ball
Follow-Through • Weight remains back • Weak follow-through	• Momentum forward through point of contact • Follow-through to waist level or higher

Error Detection and Correction for Lofted Passes

Errors in passing lofted balls usually stem from one or more of the following.

1. Improper balance-foot placement
2. Improper kicking-foot position
3. Improper ball contact

Closely observe these three aspects of performance. And because beginning students sometimes hesitate to drive the foot beneath the ball for fear of kicking the ground, they often fail to generate height on the pass. But practice of proper technique usually alleviates this problem.

ERROR ⊘   **CORRECTION**

Short Chip Pass

1. The ball fails to clear an opponent standing between the passer and the target.

2. The pass lacks accuracy.

1. Tell the student to place the balance foot beside the ball and point it toward the target and drive the instep of the kicking foot beneath the ball with a short, powerful motion.

2. Tell the student to contact the ball with the full lower instep and square the shoulders with the intended target.

Long Chip Pass

1. The pass falls short of the target.

2. The pass lacks accuracy.

1. Have the student use a greater follow-through and plant the balance foot to the side, slightly behind the ball. The student should lean slightly backward and extend the firmly positioned kicking foot as the leg is drawn back.

2. Tell the student to firmly position the kicking foot and square the shoulders to the target as the ball is kicked. The instep of the foot should contact the lower half of the ball's vertical midline.

Receiving Lofted Ball With Instep Rating

BEGINNING LEVEL	ADVANCED LEVEL
Preparation	
• Shoulders at angle to oncoming ball	• Body and shoulders square with oncoming ball
• Receiving foot planted on ground	• Receiving foot raised 12 to 18 inches off ground
• Receiving foot somewhat flexed and wobbly	• Receiving foot extended and parallel to ground
• Balance leg stiff and straight	• Balance leg flexed at knee
• Vision focused on field or opponent rather than on ball	• Head steady with vision focused on ball

(Cont.)

BEGINNING LEVEL	ADVANCED LEVEL
Execution	
• Ball received near end of foot • Foot unstable at ball impact • Receiving foot remains stationary at impact • Ball bounces up	• Ball received on center of instep • Foot firmly positioned • Receiving foot withdrawn downward on impact • Ball drops at feet in range of control
Follow-Through	
• Head down with vision on ball	• Head up with vision on full field

Receiving Lofted Ball With Thigh Rating

BEGINNING LEVEL	ADVANCED LEVEL
Preparation	
• Body to side of descending ball • Receiving leg moves upward as ball arrives • Balance leg straight and balance uncertain • Vision focused on field or opponent rather than on ball	• Body beneath descending ball • Receiving leg positioned when ball arrives • Balance leg flexed and balance good • Head steady with vision focused on ball
Execution	
• Receiving thigh at downward angle to ground at contact • Ball contacted forward on thigh, near knee • Thigh remains rigidly positioned on contact • Ball bounces up	• Receiving thigh parallel to ground at contact • Ball received on central thigh • Thigh withdrawn downward to cushion impact • Ball drops to feet in range of control
Follow-Through	
• Ball left unprotected from opponent • Head down with vision on ball	• Ball controlled away from opponent • Head up with vision on surrounding field

Receiving Lofted Ball With Chest Rating

BEGINNING LEVEL	ADVANCED LEVEL
Preparation	
• Body and shoulders at angle to flight of ball • Upper body arched far backward • Arms tight to sides • Vision focused on field or opponent rather than on ball	• Body and shoulders square with flight of ball • Upper body arched slightly backward • Arms out to sides for balance • Head steady with vision focused on ball
Execution	
• Chest unmoving at impact • Controls ball into space occupied by opponent	• Upper body withdraws slightly as ball contacts • Upper body angled to control ball into space away from opponent
Follow-Through	
• Leaves ball open to opponent • Head down with limited field vision	• Shields ball from opponent • Head up with good field vision

Receiving Lofted Ball With Head Rating

BEGINNING LEVEL	ADVANCED LEVEL
Preparation	
• Prepares late to jump • Body position shifting prior to jump • Vision on field or opponent rather than on ball	• Prepares early to jump with knees flexed and arms extended back to sides • Minimal body movement prior to jump • Head steady with vision on ball
Execution	
• Player still moving up as ball contacts head • Upper body too erect • Eyes closed as ball contacts head • Ball received on top of head • Head remains rigidly positioned at impact	• Player jumps early and meets ball at highest point of jump • Upper body arched backward • Head steady, eyes open, and vision focused on ball • Ball received on flat of forehead • Head withdrawn backward to cushion impact
Follow-Through	
• Ball bounces up off head • Lands off balance • Leaves ball open to opponent	• Ball drops to ground in range of control • Lands on both feet with balance and control • Shields ball from opponent

Error Detection and Correction for Receiving Lofted Balls

To successfully receive and control a lofted ball, a player must

1. select the proper receiving surface,
2. position the receiving surface prior to ball arrival,
3. cushion the impact by withdrawing the receiving surface, and

4. drop the ball to the ground in range of control.

Failure in one or more of these critical performance aspects results in errors when receiving lofted balls.

ERROR   **CORRECTION**

Receiving a Lofted Ball With Instep

1. The ball bounces up off the instep.

   1. Tell the student to raise the receiving foot 12 to 18 inches off the ground prior to ball arrival and withdraw the instep downward at contact.

2. The ball spins back into player's body.

   2. Tell the student to fully extend the receiving foot parallel to the ground as the ball contacts the instep. With the foot in this position the ball will drop downward with little or no spin.

Receiving a Lofted Ball With Thigh

1. The ball bounces up off the thigh.

   1. Tell the student to raise the receiving thigh parallel with the ground prior to ball arrival and as the ball arrives withdraw thigh down to cushion impact.

2. The ball bounces forward out of range of control.

   2. The student is receiving the ball too far forward on the thigh. Instruct the student to receive the ball on the central thigh, midway between the knee and hip.

3. The ball skids sideways off the thigh.

   3. The student has failed to concentrate and focus vision on the ball. Tell the student to steady his or her head and focus vision on the ball until it contacts the thigh.

Receiving a Lofted Ball With Chest

1. The ball rebounds off the chest.

   1. Tell the player to angle the upper body backward to cushion the impact as the ball arrives.

ERROR

CORRECTION

2. The ball skips off the student's chest and over his or her head.

2. The student has angled his or her upper body too far backward. Tell the student to arch backward just enough to cushion the impact of the ball.

Receiving a Lofted Ball With the Head

1. The ball bounces upward rather than dropping to the player's feet.

1. The student jumped late and is still moving at contact. Tell the student to jump early so that the ball arrives as he or she begins to descend.

2. The ball glances off the side of the player's head.

2. Tell the player to receive the ball on the large flat surface of the forehead, keeping head steady and vision on the ball.

Lofted Ball Passing and Receiving Drills

1. Short Chip to Chest
[Corresponds to *Soccer*, Step 2, Drill 1]

Group Management and Safety Tip
- Allow 5 yards between groups.

Equipment
- 1 ball per student pair

Instructions to Class
- "Select a partner and face each other at 4 to 5 yards."
- "Chip a ball back and forth. Receive each pass with your chest, drop the ball to the ground in range of control, and, once the ball is stationary, chip it back."
- "Chip pass 25 times with each foot."

Student Option
- "You may alternate the chipping foot every other pass or attempt 25 consecutive passes with one foot and then 25 with the other."

Student Keys to Success

Passing
- Square shoulders to partner.
- Drive instep beneath ball.
- Use short powerful leg snap.
- Use minimal follow-through.

Receiving

- Arch upper body backward.
- Receive ball on upper chest.
- Withdraw chest to cushion impact as ball contacts.

Student Success Goals

- 20 of 25 balls chipped with each foot to partner's chest
- 40 of 50 balls received on chest and dropped to ground in range of control

To Decrease Difficulty

- Increase distance between partners to 6 yards to lessen the upward trajectory of the ball.

To Increase Difficulty

- Decrease distance between players to 3 yards to steepen the upward trajectory of the ball.
- Require players to chip a rolling ball to partner's chest.

2. *Grid-to-Grid Chip*
[Corresponds to *Soccer*, Step 2, Drill 3]

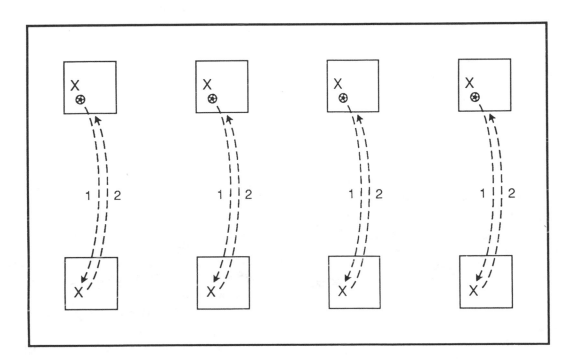

Group Management and Safety Tips

- Conduct the drill on a full-size soccer or football field.
- Instruct students to self-pace the drill.
- Use cones or flags to mark off two rows of 10-by-10-yard grids (approximately 25 yards between rows).

Equipment

- 1 ball per student pair
- Cones, flags, or similar markers to outline grid areas

Instructions to Class

- ''Select a partner and position within grids opposite each other and 25 yards apart.''

- "Chip a ball back and forth between your grids. Award yourself 2 points for a pass that drops directly into your partner's grid and 1 point for a ball that bounces there on one hop."
- "Also award yourself 1 point for each ball that you receive out of the air using 3 or fewer touches."
- "Total your points to measure your success."
- "Execute 50 chip passes per partner, 25 with each foot."

Student Option

- "Decrease or increase the distance between grids depending on your chipping ability."

Student Keys to Success

Passing

- Square shoulders to target.
- Drive foot beneath ball.
- Use complete follow-through.

Receiving

- Align body with ball.
- Select receiving surface.
- Withdraw receiving surface as ball arrives.
- Drop the ball to ground in range of control.

Student Success Goals

- 70 or more points for passing
- 40 or more points for receiving

To Decrease Difficulty

- Reduce distance between grids.
- Increase grid size.
- Allow more touches to control the ball.

To Increase Difficulty

- Increase the distance between grids.
- Decrease grid size.
- Allow only two touches to receive and control ball out of the air.

3. Pass and Receive in Threes
[Corresponds to *Soccer*, Step 2, Drill 4]

Group Management and Safety Tips

- Position groups at least 5 yards apart.
- Allow players to self-pace the drill unless they obviously lack skill, in which case instruct players to pass simultaneously at your command.

Equipment

- 2 balls per group of 3 students

Instructions to Class

- "Divide into groups of three."

- "Two students (servers) each take a ball and face one another 25 yards apart while the third student positions midway between them."
- "Servers alternate chipping their ball to the central player who receives the ball out of the air, controls it and chips it back to the server. The central player receives 15 passes from each server and then switches places with one of the servers. Repeat the exercise."
- "Receive and control the ball in only three touches."
- "Continue the drill until each player chips and receives 30 balls."

Student Options

- ''Increase or decrease the number of repetitions depending upon the available time.''
- ''Servers may chip either a stationary or rolling ball, depending upon their ability.''

Student Keys to Success

Passing

- Square shoulders to target.
- Drive foot beneath ball.
- Use short, powerful kick.
- Use minimal follow-through.

Receiving

- Control the ball out of the air.
- Select the receiving surface early.
- Position the receiving surface before the ball arrives.
- Withdraw receiving surface upon contact.
- Drop the ball to ground in range of feet.

Student Success Goals

Servers

- 25 of 30 balls chipped so that central player can receive them out of the air

Central Player

- 25 of 30 balls received and controlled with three or fewer touches

To Decrease Difficulty

- Move players closer.
- Allow more touches.

To Increase Difficulty

- Increase the distance between players.
- Strictly limit players to two touches to receive and control each pass.

4. Chip a Rolling Ball

[Corresponds to *Soccer*, Step 2, Drill 5]

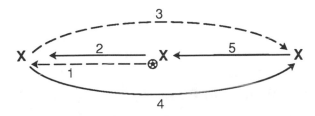

Group Management and Safety Tips

- Position groups at least 5 yards apart.
- Allow players to self-pace the drill.

Equipment

- 1 ball per group of 3 students

Instructions to Class

- ''Divide into groups of three.''
- ''Two players face one another 25 yards apart while the third player positions with a ball midway between the end players.''
- ''The central player rolls the ball to an end player, who chips it over the central player's head to the other end player. Then players rotate positions: The central player takes the position of the player who chipped the ball, who has followed the pass to the position of the receiver, who in turn has moved to the central position.''
- ''Alternate the chipping foot.''
- ''Use three or fewer touches to control the ball out of the air.''
- ''Repeat the drill until each player has passed and received 40 balls.''

Student Options

- ''As a warm-up, the end player may chip a stationary ball over the central player, and then players rotate positions.''
- ''If you are unable to chip a rolling ball with either foot, use your dominant, or strongest, foot for this drill. We will try to develop your weaker foot with a more basic drill.''

Student Keys to Success

Passing

- Square shoulders to target.
- Keep head steady with vision on ball.
- Drive foot beneath ball.
- Follow-through sufficiently to drive the ball 25 yards.

Receiving

- Align body with oncoming ball.
- Select receiving surface early.
- Position receiving surface before ball arrives.
- Withdraw receiving surface with ball contact.
- Drop ball to ground in range of feet.

Student Success Goals

- 20 of 40 balls accurately chipped over the central player's head to the classmate 25 yards away (the ball must land within 5 feet of the classmate to be considered accurate)
- 30 of 40 lofted balls received and controlled using three or fewer touches

To Decrease Difficulty

- Decrease the distance between players.
- Permit players to chip a stationary ball.
- Decrease the Success Goals.

To Increase Difficulty

- Increase the distance between players.
- Count as accurate only passes that can be controlled directly out of the air by the receiver.
- Allow only two touches to receive and control the ball.
- Increase the Success Goals.

5. *Team Tennis*
[Corresponds to *Soccer*, Step 2, Drill 6]

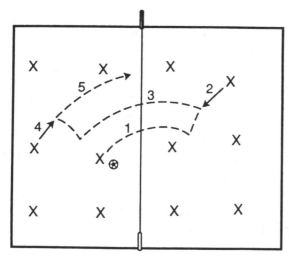

Equipment

- 1 soccer ball per game
- 1 tennis or volleyball net and posts per game. If nets are unavailable, string a rope between two poles to serve as the net.

Instructions to Class

- "Divide into teams of six."
- "Position one team on each side of the net."
- "One team starts by having a player serve (chip) a stationary ball over the net from the team's endline into the opponents' court. The receiving team may receive the ball directly out of the air or let it bounce once. The receiving player must control the ball with one touch and with a second touch play it either over the net or to a teammate. Teammates may pass the ball to one another through the air before returning it. But once received, the ball must not touch the ground before returning to the opponent's court."

Group Management and Safety Tips

- Divide students into equal teams. Place two teams on a court.
- Set up the nets and courts prior to class.
- Caution players not to collide with teammates when receiving a ball.

- "You may use your feet or head to propel the ball over the net and any skills we have practiced to receive and control the ball."
- "If the receiving team fails to return the serve before the ball bounces twice or plays the ball out of bounds, the serving team retains service and receives 1 point."
- "Change of service occurs when the ball is served out of the playing court or the serving team fails to properly receive the return of service. Only the serving team can score points."
- "The first team to score 15 points wins. Play best of five games."

Student Options

- "Serve the ball with either foot."
- "If the games run long play best of three."

Student Keys to Success

- Focus on serve height and accuracy.
- Develop communication and teamwork.

Team Success Goal

- 15 points scored before opponents.

To Decrease Difficulty

- Increase players per team.
- Lower the net.
- Allow ball to bounce twice before returning over the net.
- Enlarge the court.
- Allow players to serve by dropping the ball from their hands and volleying it over the net.

To Increase Difficulty

- Raise the net.
- Reduce the court.
- Require players to serve by chipping a rolling ball.

6. Numbers Passing Game
[Corresponds to *Soccer*, Step 2, Drill 7]

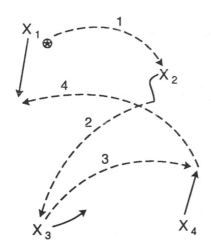

Group Management and Safety Tips

- If several groups are playing in the same area, caution students to avoid collision by keeping their heads up and watching the field.
- Encourage verbal communication among students.

- If the class does not divide evenly into groups of four, one or two groups can have three or five players.

Equipment

- 1 ball per group of 4 students

Instructions to Class

- "Divide into groups of four."
- "In each group number yourselves 1, 2, 3, and 4 and spread out in a large field area. (Number to three or five in odd-sized groups.) Player 1 begins the drill with the ball."
- "The student with the ball chips it through the air to the player numbered above him or her. For example, Player 1 chips to Player 2, Player 2 to 3, and so on. Player 4 completes the circuit by chipping to Player 1. Meanwhile, all players remain in constant motion."
- "Try to receive and control the ball directly out of the air."

- "Continue until each player has passed and received 25 balls. At least 20 of your passes should be receivable directly out of the air. Try to receive and control the ball using only two touches."

Student Option

- "Use either foot to chip the ball."

Student Keys to Success

Passing

- Square shoulders with target.
- Drive foot beneath ball.
- Adjust follow-through to suit the distance the ball must travel.
- Impart slight backspin on the ball.

Receiving

- Move to where the ball will drop and receive it out of the air.
- Withdraw the receiving surface as the ball arrives.
- Drop the ball to ground in range of control.

Student Success Goals

- 20 of 25 accurate chip passes to a moving classmate
- 80% of accurate chips received and controlled to ground using two or fewer touches

To Decrease Difficulty

- Move players closer.
- Allow players to chip a stationary ball.
- Allow an unlimited number of touches to control the ball.
- Decrease the movement speed from a jog to a fast walk.
- Decrease the Success Goal.

To Increase Difficulty

- Spread players further.
- Require that players chip a rolling ball.
- Increase the movement speed from a jog to a run.
- Require players to chip with their weakest foot.
- Increase the Success Goal.

7. *Throw, Receive and Catch*
[New Drill]

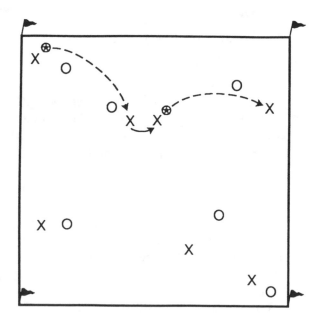

Group Management and Safety Tips

- Divide students into teams of six to eight.
- Use cones, flags, or similar markers to outline a 30-by-35-yard playing area for each game.

Equipment

- Cones, flags, or similar markers
- Colored scrimmage vests to differentiate teams
- 1 ball per game

Instructions to Class

- "Divide into teams of six to eight. Two teams position in each playing field. One team has the ball."

- "The team with the ball tries to retain it by interpassing; the opposing team tries to steal the ball. Players interpass by throwing (not kicking) the ball to a teammate, who receives and controls it with chest, thigh, instep, or head, as appropriate. After receiving and controlling the ball the player takes it in his or her hands (before it hits ground) and passes to another teammate."
- "Players can take no more than five steps with the ball before passing. The defending team can gain possession by intercepting passes or picking up a dropped ball. Defending players cannot wrestle the ball from an opponent."
- "When a team completes 10 consecutive passes without allowing the ball to be stolen, it scores 1 point. Play for 15 minutes. The team scoring the most points wins."

Student Option

- None

Student Keys to Success

- Select the receiving surface early.
- Line up with the oncoming ball.
- Cushion the ball impact by withdrawing the receiving surface.
- Catch the ball in your hands after controlling it.

Student Success Goals

- Receive and control each ball tossed to you.
- Help your team score more points than opponents.

To Decrease Difficulty

- Count 1 point scored for five consecutive passes among teammates.

To Increase Difficulty

- Count 1 point scored for 15 consecutive passes among teammates.

Step 3 Individual Ball Possession

Each player must master the skills of maintaining ball possession. Dribbling and shielding are essential to that aim. By dribbling, individuals move the ball on the field and effectively penetrate opposing defenses to create scoring opportunities. Shielding skills protect the ball from challenging opponents. To shield the ball, a player crouches, positions sideways to the opponent, and controls the ball with the foot farthest from the opponent. By adding body feints and other deceptive movements the attacker can confuse the defender.

Unlike most soccer skills, dribbling is not restricted to one correct method. Players can develop their own style and flair so long as they beat an opponent while maintaining ball possession. However, the situation often dictates the type of dribbling used: dribbling for close control in a crowd of players or dribbling for speed in open space. When dribbling for close control, students couple sudden changes of speed and direction with deceptive body feints. When dribbling for speed, students push the ball 2 or 3 yards ahead, sprint to it, and push it again. Encourage students to push the ball forward with either the instep or its outside portion.

Emphasize the basic principles that determine when and where to dribble during a game. In general, players should not take on (i.e., dribble at) opponents in the defending third of the field where loss of ball possession may result in an opponents' score. If a player takes on and beats an opponent in the attacking third of the field nearest the opponent's goal, however, he or she has created a scoring opportunity. And if the player is stripped of the ball, opposing players must still travel the length of the field to score.

Dribble for Close Control Rating

BEGINNING LEVEL	ADVANCED LEVEL
Preparation	
• Body erect and rigid • Balance poor • Vision focused solely on ball	• Body semicrouched • Low center of gravity, solid base of support • Head up with vision on surrounding area and players
Execution	
• Dribble at consistent speed in consistent direction • Movements very predictable • Uses toes to control ball • Dribbles into opponent	• Uses sudden changes of speed and direction • Uses deceptive body movements to unbalance opponent • Uses inside or outside surfaces of the feet to control ball • Reacts to opponent movements, controls ball in space away from opponent

(Cont.)

BEGINNING LEVEL	ADVANCED LEVEL
Follow-Through	
• Ball travels far from feet	• Keeps ball under body in close control of feet
• Head down with vision focused solely on ball	• Head up with vision on field; looks at ball only to push it again

Dribble for Speed Rating

BEGINNING LEVEL	ADVANCED LEVEL
Preparation	
• Body low semicrouched	• Body more erect than when dribbling for close control
• Ball beneath body and between feet	• Ball ahead of player
• Head down with vision focused solely on ball	• Head up with vision on field
Execution	
• Ball close to feet	• Ball pushed ahead into open space
• Uses short, choppy steps	• Uses long strides to sprint to ball
• Pushes ball forward with toe; has poor control	• Pushes ball forward with instep or outside surface of instep
Follow-Through	
• Slow acceleration	• Quick acceleration after pushing ball into space
• Head down with vision focused solely on ball	• Head up with vision on field

Error Detection and Correction for Dribbling Skills

Because the objectives of dribbling for close control differ from those of dribbling for speed, performance errors will also differ. With both skills, however, loss of possession is the most critical error. Provide practice of both types of dribbling skills to prepare students for any game situation.

ERROR 🚫   **CORRECTION**

Dribble for Close Control

1. The ball rolls out of the student's range of control.

2. Student focuses vision solely on the ball.

1. Tell the student to keep the ball under his or her body and control it with either the inside or outside surfaces of the feet. This position allows the student to quickly change speed and direction while maintaining control of the ball.

2. Tell the student to watch nearby opponents and teammates, and look down only when preparing to push the ball. Emphasize that the head be up and vision on the surrounding field at all other times.

Dribble for Speed

1. Player pushes the ball forward with inside surface of foot.

2. Player dribbles the ball too close to the feet.

1. Have the student push the ball forward with the instep or outside surface of the foot, which is a more natural running motion and far less awkward.

2. Failure to push the ball forward into open space results in short, choppy steps and a lack of speed. Tell the player to push the ball far enough ahead that he or she can strike forward at top speed to catch it before pushing it again.

Shielding Rating

BEGINNING LEVEL	ADVANCED LEVEL
Preparation	
• Stands erect • Positions with back to opponent • Vision focused solely on ball	• Crouches with wide base of support • Positions sideways to opponent • Head is up with vision on opponent
Execution	
• Arms held tight to sides • Ball between player's feet • Consistent, predictable movement	• Arms held away from body for improved balance • Ball controlled with foot farthest from opponent • Uses body feints and quick directional changes to unbalance opponent

(Cont.)

BEGINNING LEVEL	ADVANCED LEVEL
Follow-Through • Unaware of changing position of opponent • Allows space between ball and opponent to close	• Repositions body in response to movement of opponent • Repositions body to maintain distance between ball and opponent

Error Detection and Correction for Shielding Skills

Shielding errors usually result in loss of the ball. Most errors stem from incorrect body position. Closely observe how students position their bodies in relation to the ball and opponent. Players must constantly readjust position to maintain sufficient distance between the ball and opponent.

ERROR

CORRECTION

1. The opponent can reach in with his or her leg and poke the ball away.

2. The player stands too erect.

1. Tell the student to create the greatest possible distance between the ball and challenging opponent. He or she should position sideways and control the ball with the foot farthest from the opponent.

2. Have the player crouch with feet approximately shoulder-width apart. Explain how a wide base of support provides stability and allows the player to maintain the greatest distance between the ball and opponent.

Dribbling and Shielding Drills

1. Individual Dribble
[Corresponds to *Soccer*, Step 3, Drill 1]

Group Management and Safety Tips

• All students dribble simultaneously in a designated field area of approximately 30-by-30 yards.

• Caution students to avoid collisions with one another.
• Begin the drill at a slow pace and increase the speed as players become more confident.

Equipment

- 1 ball per student

Instructions to Class

- "Get a ball and dribble in random fashion in the field."
- "Use the inside, outside, and instep of your feet to control the ball. Quickly change speed and direction as you dribble."
- "Keep your head up with vision on the field to avoid collisions."
- "Dribble until you have touched the ball a minimum of 150 times with various surfaces of your feet."

Student Options

- "Increase speed as you feel more comfortable, but don't dribble so fast that you lose control."
- "Alternate dribbling for close control and for speed, depending upon the available space and the location of classmates."

Student Keys to Success

- Keep ball in range of control.
- Quickly change speed and direction.
- Use deceptive body feints.
- Keep head up with vision on the field area.

Student Success Goal

- 150 touches of the ball without its rolling into the path of another student or outside of the playing area

To Decrease Difficulty

- Increase size of area so students have more open space in which to maneuver.
- Decrease the drill speed; have players dribble at a slow jog.
- Decrease the Success Goal.

To Increase Difficulty

- Decrease size of area so players must dribble in confined space.
- Increase speed of drill to simulate game condition.

2. Shadow Dribbling
[Corresponds to *Soccer*, Step 3, Drill 2]

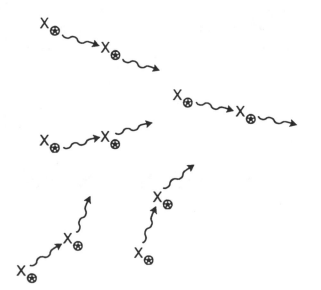

Group Management and Safety Tips

- All students dribble simultaneously in a designated field area of approximately 40-by-50 yards.
- Caution students to avoid collisions.
- Begin the drill at a slow pace and increase the speed as players become more confident.

Equipment

- 1 ball per student

Instructions to Class

- "Get a ball and select a partner."

- ''Designate one partner as the leader, the other as the shadow. The leader can dribble anywhere within the playing area; the shadow tries to closely follow and mimic the leader's dribbling movements. Meanwhile the leader tries to lose the shadow through deceptive body movements and quick changes of speed and direction.''
- ''The leader receives 1 point each time he or she loses the shadow (creates a 3-yard space between them).''
- ''Dribble continuously for 4 minutes. I'll blow the whistle to begin and end the drill. After a short rest partners will switch roles and repeat the drill.''

Student Option

- ''Dribble for close control, speed, or both.''

Student Keys to Success

Leader

- Quickly change speed and direction.
- Use deceptive body movements.
- Control ball.

Shadow

- Keep head up and vision on leader.
- Control ball.

Student Success Goal

- 10 points or more as leader

To Decrease Difficulty

- Award 1 point to leader each time he or she creates a 2-yard space between them.
- Shorten drill to 2 minutes.
- Decrease the Success Goal.

To Increase Difficulty

- Award 1 point to leader each time he or she creates a 4-yard space between them.
- Lengthen the drill to 6 minutes.
- Increase the Success Goal.

3. *Slalom Dribble*

[Corresponds to *Soccer*, Step 3, Drill 3]

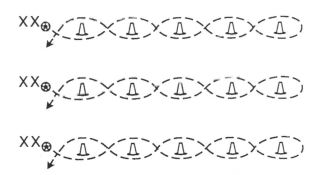

Group Management and Safety Tips

- Set up one slalom course per two students.
- Set up slalom courses at least 5 yards apart so that players from adjacent groups do not interfere with each other.
- Use five markers (cones) positioned in a straight line with 2 yards between them for each course.
- For an odd number of students have one group of three.

Equipment

- 1 ball per 2 students
- Cones, flags, or similar markers to designate the slalom courses

Instructions to Class

- ''Divide into groups of two and position in front of a slalom course.''
- ''Take turns dribbling through the course. Dribble alternately around the left and right of each cone to the end of the course, then turn around and repeat the pattern back to the starting point. Exchange the ball with your partner and rest while he or she dribbles through the course.''
- ''For each time you complete the slalom without knocking down a cone, award yourself 1 point.''
- ''Continue taking turns until each of you has completed 20 repetitions for 20 possible points each.''

Student Options

- "Organize the slalom in a circle or curve rather than a straight line."
- "Dribble at half speed for the first couple repetitions to become accustomed to the course."

Student Keys to Success

- Keep close control of ball at all times.
- Keep head up with vision on course whenever possible.
- Quickly change direction to cut in and out of cones.

Student Success Goal

- 18 of 20 points

To Decrease Difficulty

- Move markers farther apart.
- Reduce number of markers.
- Reduce the Success Goal.

To Increase Difficulty

- Move markers closer together.
- Require students to dribble through course at top speed.
- Increase numbers of markers.

4. Cone to Cone
[Corresponds to *Soccer*, Step 3, Drill 4]

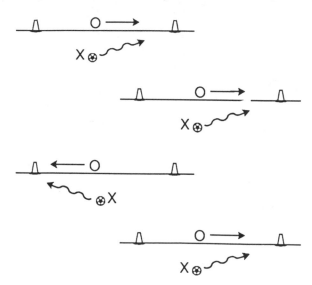

Group Management and Safety Tips

- Position two cones 10 yards apart for each student pair. Use tape or chalk to mark a straight line between the cones.
- Position groups at least 5 yards apart.

Equipment

- 1 ball per student pair
- 2 cones or markers per student pair

Instructions to Class

- "Choose a partner and share a ball."

- "Center yourselves between two markers and face each other across the line. One player, the dribbler, begins the drill with the ball."
- "The dribbler tries to dribble laterally to one cone or the other before his or her partner (defender) can get there. The dribbler uses body feints, deceptive movements, and changes of speed or direction to unbalance the defender. Neither player may cross the line during the exercise."
- "The dribbler receives 1 point for each time he or she beats the defender to a cone."
- "Play for 2 minutes, then rest. Change roles and repeat the drill. I will signal the beginning and end of each 2-minute period."

Student Option

- "Warm up at half speed against an imaginary opponent."

Student Keys to Success

Dribbler

- Use sudden speed and direction changes.
- Use body feints to unbalance the defender.
- Quickly accelerate with ball.
- Keep close control of ball.

Defender

- Maintain good balance.
- Crouch.
- Watch the ball.

Student Success Goal

- 5 or more points scored in a 2-minute game

To Decrease Difficulty

- Decrease distance between cones to 5 yards.
- Decrease the Success Goal.

To Increase Difficulty

- Increase distance between cones to 15 yards.
- Increase the Success Goal.

5. *Soccer Marbles*

[Corresponds to *Soccer*, Step 3, Drill 5]

Group Management and Safety Tips

- Several groups can play in a large field area.
- Caution students to avoid collisions.
- Caution students to avoid stepping on stray balls from other groups.

Equipment

- 1 ball per student

Instructions to Class

- "Divide into groups of three. Each player should have a ball."
- "Designate one player in your group as 'it.' The player who is 'it' may dribble anywhere within the playing area. The other two group members dribble in close pursuit and pass their balls to hit the 'it' player's ball. The 'it' player is penalized 1 point for each time his or her ball is hit by another player's ball."
- "If you are 'it' quickly change speed and direction to elude the chasers."
- "Play the game for 3 minutes, then designate another player as 'it.' I will signal the start and stop of each 3-minute period."

Student Option

- "Chasers can use either inside-of-the-foot or outside-of-the-foot passes."

Student Keys to Success

- Change speed and direction suddenly to elude the chasers.
- Shield the ball with your body.
- Keep your head up as much as possible with good field vision.

Student Success Goal

- 5 or fewer penalty points for player who is "it"

To Decrease Difficulty

- Require chasers to share one ball between them.
- Use one chaser instead of two.

To Increase Difficulty

- Reduce the size of the playing area to restrict the player who is "it."
- Use three chasers instead of two.

6. *Speed Dribble Relay*

[Corresponds to *Soccer*, Step 3, Drill 6]

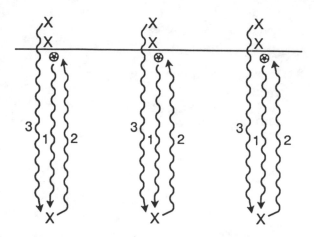

Group Management and Safety Tips

- Position groups at least 5 yards apart.
- Depending upon the number in the class, one group may have more or fewer than three players.

Equipment

- 1 ball per group of 3 players

Instructions to Class

- "Divide into groups of three. Two players in each group stand on the goal line (one with a ball). The third player faces them 30 yards away."
- "One of the players on the goal line begins the drill by dribbling at top speed and exchanging the ball with the player 30 yards away."

- "The player who received the ball immediately dribbles back to the starting point and exchanges the ball with the third player in the group. Continue the relay until each player has dribbled the 30 yard distance 20 times."
- "Award yourself 1 point each time you dribble the ball at top speed and exchange the ball without error."

Student Option

- "Use either the instep or outside surface of the instep to push the ball forward."

Student Keys to Success

- Push the ball ahead and sprint to it.
- Keep head up and vision on field.
- Slow down when exchanging the ball.

Student Success Goal

- 18 of 20 possible points

To Decrease Difficulty

- Decrease dribbling distance.
- Perform drill at half speed.
- Reduce the Success Goal.

To Increase Difficulty

- Increase dribbling distance.
- Add an extra player to chase the dribbler from behind.

7. *Dribble and Shield in the Grid*

[Corresponds to *Soccer*, Step 3, Drill 7]

Group Management and Safety Tips

- Use cones or flags to outline a 10-by-10-yard area for each student pair.
- Keep at least 5 yards between grids.
- Caution students to stay out of other grids when chasing stray balls.

Equipment

- 1 ball per student pair
- Cones, flags, or other markers to outline areas

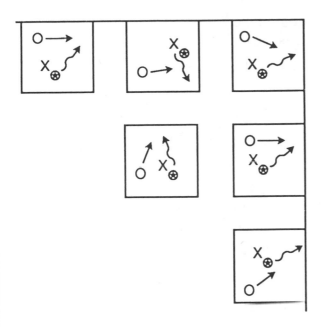

Instructions to Class

- "Choose a partner and position in one of the grids. One player begins with the ball."
- "The player with the ball dribbles and shields it from the partner (defender) in the grid."
- "The defender applies only passive pressure. Do not try to steal the ball but apply enough pressure that the player with the ball must constantly readjust to protect it."
- "Continue for 90 seconds, then rest and reverse roles. I will signal the start and end of each 90-second period."

- "The shielding player is penalized 1 point for each time the ball leaves the grid area or rolls more than 3 feet from his or her feet."
- "Each player will take five turns at shielding the ball."

Student Option

- "Execute the drill at half speed until you gain confidence."

Student Keys to Success

- Position sideways between ball and defender.
- Control ball with foot farthest from defender.
- Always move away from pressure of defender.
- Change speed and direction suddenly to unbalance defender.

Student Success Goal

- Fewer than 3 penalty points in each 90-second drill

To Decrease Difficulty

- Increase grid size.

To Increase Difficulty

- Decrease grid size.
- Have the defender apply maximum pressure and attempt to steal the ball.

8. Score by Dribbling Only
[New Drill]

Group Management and Safety Tips

- Use cones or flags to outline a 40-by-50-yard area for each game.
- Divide class into equal teams of six to eight students.
- Prohibit slide tackles.

Equipment

- Cones or flags to mark the area
- Colored scrimmage vests to differentiate teams
- 1 ball per game

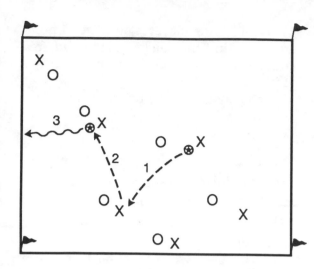

Instructions to Class

- "Two teams position on opposite halves of the field."
- "The game begins with a kickoff from the center of the playing area. Follow regular soccer rules except that you score 1 point by dribbling over the opponent's endline rather than by shooting: The entire end-line is the goal line. Play for 20 minutes and total the points scored for each team."

Student Option

- None

Student Keys to Success

- Maintain ball possession.
- Use interpassing of the ball among teammates.
- Use creative dribbling in attacking third of the field.

Team Success Goal

- More points scored than opponents.

To Decrease Difficulty

- Increase field size to provide students more space.
- Reduce team size.

To Increase Difficulty

- Decrease field size to provide students less space.
- Increase team size.

9. Game With Restricted Dribbling
[New Drill]

Group Management and Safety Tips

- Use cones or similar markers to divide the field into three equal zones. Position a regulation goal on each endline.
- Organize the class in two equal teams.

Equipment

- Cones or similar markers
- 1 ball per game
- Colored scrimmage vests to differentiate teams

Instructions to Class

- "Each team will defend a goal and try to score in the opponent's goal. The game will start with a kickoff from the center of the field. I will award one team the ball to begin the game."
- "Follow regular soccer rules except for the following zone restrictions. Players may use only one- and two-touch passing in the defending third of the field: Dribbling

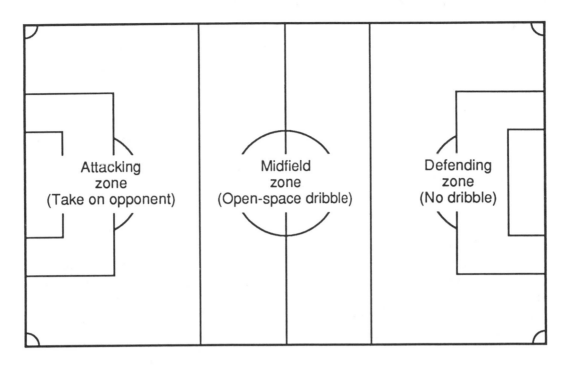

Attacking
zone
(Take on opponent)

Midfield
zone
(Open-space dribble)

Defending
zone
(No dribble)

is prohibited in the defending third. In the midfield zone players may dribble in open space but cannot dribble at (take on) an opponent. Dribbling is required in the attacking zone of the field. In that area the player with the ball must dribble at and beat an opponent before passing to a teammate or shooting at the goal. Players who violate a zone restriction lose the ball to the opposing team.''

- ''Play for 20 minutes. Keep total of the goals scored.''

Student Option

- None

Student Keys to Success

- Maintain ball possession.
- Change the point of attack.
- Take on opponent in the attacking third of the field.

Team Success Goal

- More points scored than opponents.

To Decrease Difficulty

- Increase the area to provide students with more space and time.

To Increase Difficulty

- Decrease the area to provide students less space and time.

Step 4 Gaining Possesion of the Ball

Although soccer is a team sport, individual contests (one versus one) regularly occur in game play. Therefore, all players must learn to defend as well as attack individually. Your students already know the dribbling and shielding skills used to maintain ball possession. Now teach them the defensive skills used to gain ball possession from an opponent: the block, poke, and slide tackles.

Tell students to use the block tackle whenever possible because it provides more body control than the poke or slide tackles. The block tackle works best when an opponent is dribbling directly at a player. Instruct students to use the poke tackle when approaching the dribbler from the side. Caution students to avoid making physical contact with the dribbler prior to poking the ball away: Kicking an opponent while trying to set the ball free is a direct foul.

Introduce students to proper slide tackle technique, but emphasize that this tackle is a last resort. Because the player must leave his or her feet in a slide tackle, the player will not be positioned to catch the opponent if the ball is not set free.

Block Tackle Rating

BEGINNING LEVEL	ADVANCED LEVEL
Preparation	
• Square stance	• Staggered stance (one foot slightly ahead of other)
• Weight back on heels	• Weight centered over balls of feet
• Stands very erect	• Crouched with low center of gravity
• Focuses vision on opponent	• Vision focused on ball
Execution	
• Shoulders at angle to dribbler	• Shoulders square to dribbler
• Player leans back and extends leg to block ball	• Player drives foot into ball from crouched position
• Blocking foot uncertain or wobbly	• Blocking foot firm at contact
• Lack of power when blocking ball	• Short powerful snap of leg
Follow-Through	
• Momentum of blocking foot stops at contact	• Body weight moves forward as foot drives through point of contact
• Attacker retains ball	• Blocker gains ball

Poke Tackle Rating

BEGINNING LEVEL	ADVANCED LEVEL
Preparation	
• Uncertain body control and balance	• Good body control and balance when closing on dribbler
• Continues at high speed when nearing dribbler	• Slows when nearing dribbler
• Focuses vision on opponent	• Vision focused on ball
Execution	
• Jumps in to tackle ball	• Crouches and extends leg and foot to poke ball away
• Contacts dribbler prior to ball	• Avoids contact with dribbler when poking ball with toes
• Falls to ground after poking ball	• Withdraws blocking leg after contact with ball
Follow-Through	
• Dribbler retains ball	• Chases ball to gain possession
• Cannot recover due to poor balance and body control	• Collects ball and counterattacks

Slide Tackle Rating

BEGINNING LEVEL	ADVANCED LEVEL
Preparation	
• Uncertain body control when chasing dribbler	• Good balance and body control when chasing dribbler
• Focuses vision on opponent	• Vision focused on ball
Execution	
• Slides on back or stomach	• Slides on side to slightly ahead of ball
• Impacts ground hard	• Places arms and hands down to side to cushion impact with ground
• Contacts opponent before tackling ball	• Kicks ball away with instep
Follow-Through	
• Dribbler retains ball	• Ball set free of dribbler

Error Detection and Correction for Tackling Skills

Closely observe students as they practice the different tackling skills. Require them to maintain body control at all times. A lack of control results in missed tackles and sometimes injury to the tackler, the dribbler, or both.

Most errors occur due to poor timing or contacting the dribbler prior to the ball. Avoid such errors by teaching students to maintain good balance as they near the dribbler, then use appropriate tackling skills to win ball possession.

ERROR

CORRECTION

Block Tackle

1. Student leans backward and reaches out with leg.

2. Student's tackle attempt fails to win ball possession.

1. Have the student crouch with weight centered over the balls of the feet. From that posture he or she should snap the leg powerfully to block the ball, using the inside of the foot.

2. The blocking foot must be firmly positioned as it contacts the ball. Otherwise, the kick will lack power to successfully tackle.

Poke Tackle

1. Student fouls the dribbler.

1. Good body control and balance are essential to a successful poke tackle. Tell the student to slow when nearing the dribbler, focus on the ball, and then extend the tackling leg to poke ball away.

Slide Tackle

1. Student slides into the dribbler from behind.

2. Student slides on stomach or back.

1. Instruct student to slide to a position ahead of the dribbler and then kick the ball away with a snaplike motion of the leg.

2. Tell student to slide on his or her side, which provides greater body control and enables quicker recovery after tackling the ball.

Tackling Drills

1. Block Tackle Stationary Ball
[Corresponds to *Soccer*, Step 4, Drill 1]

Group Management and Safety Tips

- Have students start at half speed.
- Emphasize correct technique, not power.
- Have students repeat the drill at their own pace.

Equipment

- 1 ball per student pair

Instructions to Class

- "Pair up and face your partner 2 yards away."
- "One partner pins a ball to the ground with the sole of his or her foot; the other practices the block tackle on the stationary ball. Use correct form."
- "Assume a semicrouch, angle your blocking foot sideways, and then block the ball with the inside of your foot."
- "Perform 40 block tackles, 20 with each foot. Award yourself 1 point for each correct block tackle."
- "After 40 block tackles switch roles and repeat the drill."

Student Options

- "Execute 20 block tackles with your right foot, then 20 with your left foot, or alternate every other repetition."
- "Begin at half speed, then tackle at your own pace; this is not a race."

Student Keys to Success

- Assume a semicrouch with weight centered over balls of feet.
- Focus vision on the ball.
- Keep blocking foot firm.
- Block center of ball with short, powerful leg snap.

Student Success Goal

- 20 of 20 possible points with right foot
- 20 of 20 possible points with left foot

To Decrease Difficulty

- Have students walk through the drill.

To Increase Difficulty

- Require faster speed of execution.
- Have the player with the ball slowly dribble toward the tackler so that the tackler must block tackle a rolling ball.

2. Block Tackle the Dribbler
[Corresponds to *Soccer*, Step 4, Drill 2]

Group Management and Safety Tips

- Position groups at least 5 yards apart.
- Allow students to self-pace the drill.

Equipment

- 1 ball per student pair

Instructions to Class

- "Pair up and face a partner 10 yards away. One player has a ball."
- "The player with the ball dribbles toward his or her partner (defender) at half speed. The defender should close the distance and block tackle the ball at an opportune moment. The defender should maintain good body control and balance."
- "Execute 10 block tackles with each foot, switch roles with your partner, and repeat."

- "Award yourself 1 point for each successful block tackle."

Student Option

- "As the defender's confidence grows, the dribbler can increase to three-quarter speed."

Student Keys to Success

- Quickly close distance to dribbler.
- Slow down as you near dribbler.
- Maintain semicrouch with vision focused on the ball.
- Block tackle with short, powerful leg snap.

Student Success Goal

- 8 of 10 points with right foot
- 8 of 10 points with left foot

To Decrease Difficulty

- Move dribbler and defender closer.
- Require the dribbler to use a fast walk.
- Decrease the Success Goal.

To Increase Difficulty

- Move dribbler and defender farther apart.
- Allow the dribbler to dribble at full speed.
- Increase the Success Goal.

3. Line-to-Line Game

[Corresponds to *Soccer*, Step 4, Drill 3]

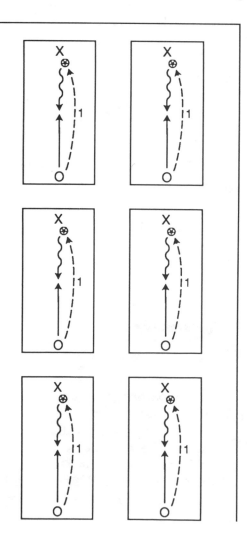

Group Management and Safety Tips

- Use cones or flags to outline a 10-by-20-yard grid for each pair of students.
- Maintain at least 5 yards between grids.

Equipment

- 1 ball per student pair
- Cones, flags, or other markers

Instructions to Class

- "Choose a partner and stand at opposite ends of a grid. One player has a ball."
- "The player with the ball passes it to his or her partner who receives and controls it, then immediately attempts to dribble the length of the grid."
- "The student who served the ball becomes the defender, closes the distance, and block or poke tackles to prevent the attacker from dribbling the length of the grid. The dribbler must stay within the side boundaries of the grid."
- "The defender receives 1 point for a successful tackle. Repeat the drill 20 times for 20 possible points, then switch roles with your partner and repeat."

Student Option

- "You can serve either ground or lofted balls to your partner."

Student Keys to Success

- Slow down when nearing the dribbler.
- Maintain continual body control and balance.
- Use the block tackle when facing the dribbler.
- Use the poke tackle when dribbler is running past you.
- Avoid contact with dribbler prior to tackling.
- Remain on feet when tackling.

Student Success Goal

- 15 of 20 possible points

To Decrease Difficulty

- Make the grid narrower to decrease maneuvering room.
- Require attacker to dribble into a small goal on opposite end of grid. This will decrease the area the tackler must defend.
- Decrease the Success Goal.

To Increase Difficulty

- Increase grid length and width so dribbler has more maneuvering room.
- Increase the Success Goal.

4. All Against All
[Corresponds to *Soccer*, Step 4, Drill 4]

Group Management and Safety Tips

- Use cones or flags to outline a 15-by-15-yard grid for each group.
- Position grids at least 5 yards apart.
- Caution students to play under control.
- Prohibit slide tackling.

Equipment

- 1 ball per student
- Cones, flags, or similar markers

Instructions to Class

- "Everyone get a soccer ball and organize into groups of four students each. One or two groups can have an uneven number of players depending on the number in the class. Position your group in one of the grids."
- "On my command—'Begin!'—dribble in random fashion in your grid. After 30 seconds or so I will say 'Go!' and you will begin playing all versus all. Protect your own ball while attempting to tackle and kick other players' balls out of the grid."
- "Award yourself 1 point for each time you tackle another player's ball and kick it out of the grid. If your ball is kicked out of the grid, quickly retrieve it, return to the grid, and continue. Total the points you score."

- "Play for 5 minutes. I will signal the end of play."

Student Options

- "Creatively combine dribbling and shielding skills to protect your ball."
- "Use either block or poke tackles to win possession of another player's ball before kicking it out of the grid. Do not use slide tackles."

Student Keys to Success

- Maintain balance and body control.
- Focus vision on opponent's ball when preparing to tackle.
- Do not contact dribbler prior to ball.
- Tackle with power and determination.
- Always protect your own ball.

Student Success Goal

- More points scored than other group members

To Decrease Difficulty

- Reduce grid size.
- Increase the number of players in each grid.

To Increase Difficulty

- Enlarge grid.
- Use fewer players per group.

5. Tackle All
[Corresponds to *Soccer*, Step 4, Drill 5]

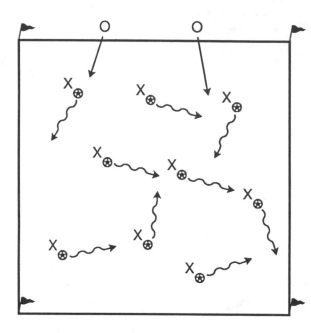

Group Management and Safety Tips

- Play in a 25-by-25-yard area. Adjust the area size depending on the class size.
- Caution defenders to always play under control.
- Use two defenders for up to 20 students. Use three or four defenders if the class is extremely large.
- Prohibit slide tackling.

Equipment

- 1 ball for every dribbler
- Cones, flags, or other markers to outline the playing area

Instructions to Class

- "Everyone can participate in this drill. We will play within a 25-by-25-yard grid."
- "I will select two defenders and position them outside the grid. All remaining students get a ball and position in the grid."

- "On my command—'Begin!'—students in the grid dribble in random fashion. On my next command—'Go!'—the defenders sprint into the grid area and try to tackle and win possession of a dribbler's ball. A defender receives 1 point for every ball he or she successfully tackles. After winning possession, the defender returns the ball to the dribbler and attempts to tackle another player's ball. Defenders cannot tackle the same player's ball twice in succession."
- "The drill ends when the first defender scores 10 points."
- "After a short rest we will repeat the drill with two new defenders."

Student Option

- "Use either block or poke tackles. Do not use slide tackles."

Student Keys to Success

- Maintain balance and body control.
- Do not become reckless in tackle attempts.
- Focus concentration on the ball.
- Tackle with power and determination.

Student Success Goal

- 10 points scored as a defender

To Decrease Difficulty

- Reduce the size of the playing area.
- Increase the number of dribblers.

To Increase Difficulty

- Increase the size of the playing area.
- Reduce the number of dribblers.

6. *Attack or Defend*
[New Drill]

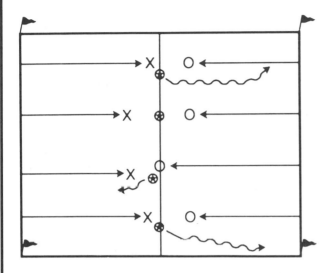

Group Management and Safety Tips

- Divide class into two equal teams.
- Use cones, flags, or similar markers to outline a 40-by-50-yard playing area. Bisect the field equally with a midline. Equally space balls along the midline, with one ball for every two players.
- Tell students to use block or poke tackles. Prohibit slide tackles. Require students to stay on their feet at all times.

Equipment

- 1 ball per 2 students
- Cones or flags to designate the playing field
- Colored scrimmage vests to differentiate teams

Instructions to Class

- "This drill uses one ball for every two players. Players from each team position along their respective endlines facing the midline, where the balls are set up."
- "On my command players sprint to the midline, compete for possession of a ball, and attempt to dribble it to their own endline. Teams score 1 point for each ball dribbled (not kicked) over the endline. Players not winning possession try to prevent opponents from scoring by tackling their soccer balls and kicking them out of the playing area."
- "We will repeat the exercise 10 times. The team that allows fewer points wins."

Student Option

- "Use either the block or poke tackle to take the ball from an opponent. Do not slide tackle."

Student Keys to Success

- Position goalside of opponent with the ball.
- Assume proper defensive stance.
- Use balance and body control.
- Stay on feet.
- Block or poke tackle the ball.

Student Success Goal

- Fewer points allowed than opponent

To Decrease Difficulty

- Narrow the field area to reduce maneuvering space.

To Increase Difficulty

- Widen the field area to increase dribbling space.

Step 5 Individual Attack and Defense Tactics

Individual performance depends upon a number of factors. Game competition requires fitness and confident skill execution under pressure. Decision making (or tactics) also plays a critical role. Teach your students tactics in a progressive manner, from basic to more complex. Begin with the basic tactical situation: one player versus one player. Teach students the terms *attacker* and *defender*: The player with the ball is the attacker, and the opponent is the defender.

Except for goalkeepers, soccer teams have no specialists. Each player must be able to individually defend as well as attack. To prepare students for one-versus-one game situations, you must teach them individual attack and defense tactics.

INDIVIDUAL ATTACK TACTICS

1. *Maintain ball possession*. The player with the ball is the first link in the chain that leads to a goal. His or her first and foremost responsibility is to maintain ball possession.

2. *Create space*. Emphasize that space equals time: The more space a player can create, the more time he or she will have for decision making and skill execution. Players should create space using deceptive body movements (feints) designed to unbalance the defender and checking runs.

3. *Turn on defender*. Encourage dribblers in the center or attacking third of the field to turn and face the opponents' goal if possible. From that position he or she will have more positive passing options.

4. *Take on defender*. After turning with the ball the attacker should immediately take on (dribble at) the defender. This action forces the defender to choose between containing the dribbler and tackling the ball.

5. *Shortest route to goal*. Emphasize that a dribbler should always take the most direct route toward goal after beating a defender on the dribble.

Individual Attack Tactics Rating

BEGINNING LEVEL	ADVANCED LEVEL
Maintain Ball Possession	
• Leaves ball open to defender • Controls ball with foot nearest to defender	• Positions to shield ball from defender • Controls ball with foot farthest from defender
Create Space	
• Moves consistently, predictably • Moves in a straight line • Constantly harried by defender	• Uses body feints and deceptive movements to confuse defender • Uses quick changes of speed and direction to unbalance defender • Creates adequate distance between self and defender

(Cont.)

BEGINNING LEVEL	ADVANCED LEVEL
Turn On Defender	
• Often misses chance to turn on defender	• Turns on defender whenever possible
• Turns on defender without enough space and loses ball	• Creates space between self and defender and quickly turns with ball
Take On Defender	
• Turns with ball and hesitates	• Turns with ball and immediately takes on defender
• Dribbles at defender but loses ball	• Beats defender on dribble
Shortest Route to Goal	
• Beats defender on dribble but defender recovers and catches up	• Takes most direct route to goal, leaving defender behind

INDIVIDUAL DEFENSE TACTICS

1. *Control/balance.* Encourage the defender to always maintain good balance and body control.

2. *Approach to ball.* Have the defender quickly close the distance to the dribbler, then slow down when nearing the ball.

3. *Defensive stance.* Have the defender crouch slightly and keep center of gravity low. Feet should be shoulder-width apart with one foot slightly forward.

4. *Marking distance.* Marking distance is the space between the defender and the attacker being marked. A skilled attacker must be marked tightly. Also, marking should tighten the closer the opponent is to the ball or the goal. Emphasize that proper marking distance depends upon the following factors:

• Ability of the opponent
• Area of the field
• Position of the ball

5. *Goalside position.* Instruct the defending player to position between the attacker and the goal. This is called goalside position.

6. *Prevent the turn.* If the attacker is facing away from the defender, the defender should keep space tight to prevent the attacker from turning with the ball.

7. *Containment.* If the attacker is facing the defender, the defender should delay the attacker's forward movement or force him or her into areas where space is limited.

8. *Tackle the ball.* At the opportune moment the defender should challenge for ball possession.

Individual Defense Tactics Rating

BEGINNING LEVEL	ADVANCED LEVEL
Control/Balance	
• Keeps legs straight and stiff	• Knees slightly flexed
• Poor balance; reacts slowly to movements of attacker	• Good balance and body control; quickly responds to movements of attacker

(Cont.)

Individual Defense Tactics Rating (Continued)

BEGINNING LEVEL	ADVANCED LEVEL
Approach to Ball • Continues at high speed when nearing dribbler	• Slows closing run and assumes proper defensive posture when nearing attacker
Defensive Stance • Stands upright • Feet parallel and squared • Focuses vision on opponent rather than on ball	• Crouches with low center of gravity • Feet in a staggered stance, one slightly ahead of other • Vision focused on ball
Marking Distance • Attacker beats defender on dribble or passes ball behind defender	• Defender maintains enough space to avoid being beaten on dribble and positions in proper goalside depth so attacker cannot pass ball forward behind defender
Goalside Position • Positions left or right of dribbler's direct route to goal	• Blocks attacker's direct route to goal
Prevent the Turn • Allows attacker to turn with ball • Marks so tightly from behind that attacker rolls off and turns ball past defender	• Tightly marks attacker to prevent turning with ball • Positions so that, if attacker turns with ball, defender can step forward and tackle
Containment • Charges forward to win ball • Beaten on dribble	• Slows forward movement of attacker • Forces attacker to dribble laterally across field
Tackle the Ball • Focuses vision on attacker's body movements • Defender misses tackle and cannot recover to catch dribbler	• Vision focused on ball • Challenges for possession at opportune moment and wins

Error Detection and Correction for Individual Attack and Defense Tactics

Tactical errors are errors in decision making: Dribbling at the wrong time or in an inappropriate area of the field are errors resulting from poor decisions. Observe students in one-versus-one situations to see if they correctly implement individual attack and defense tactics. Your comments and corrections should target decision-making errors rather than errors in skill execution.

As teacher you must improve the decision-making capabilities of your students in order to minimize tactical errors. You can accomplish that objective by providing students with a thorough understanding of the principles underlying individual attack and defense.

ERROR   **CORRECTION**

Individual Attack Tactics

1. The student fails to protect the ball from an opponent and loses possession.

2. The player attempts to face the defender and is stripped of the ball.

3. After beating an opponent on the dribble, the dribbler allows the opponent to catch up and recover to a goalside position.

1. Teach the student to position his or her body between the challenging defender and the ball.

2. Tell the student not to turn on the defender until first creating sufficient space by using body feints and directional changes.

3. Tell the dribbler to take the most direct route toward goal after beating the defender. He or she must not allow the defending player time to recover to a goalside position.

Individual Defense Tactics

1. The defender cannot quickly respond to the attacker's movements.

2. The defender allows the attacker to turn with the ball.

1. Mobility depends upon balance and body control. Make sure the student assumes the proper defensive stance: a semicrouch with a low center of gravity. Tell the student to also assume a staggered stance, with one foot slightly ahead of the other.

2. Emphasize that tight marking can prevent an opponent from turning with the ball.

ERROR ⊘	CORRECTION
3. The defender permits a penetrating pass into the space behind him or her.	3. Have the defender position to block the attacker's most direct route to goal. From a proper goalside position the defender can prevent a penetrating pass.
4. The defender overcommits when trying to tackle and is beaten on the dribble.	4. Tell the student not to challenge for possession unless fairly certain of winning the tackle. In an actual game, it is better to delay the attacker's forward movement until additional teammates can position to provide help.

Individual Attack and Defense Drills

1. Keep Away
[Corresponds to *Soccer*, Step 5, Drill 1]

Group Management and Safety Tips

- Use cones or flags to outline a 10-by-10-yard area for each pair of students.
- Keep at least 5 yards between areas.
- Caution students to watch out for classmates in other grids when retrieving a stray ball.

Equipment

- 1 ball per student pair
- Cones, flags, or other markers to outline the grids

Instructions to Class

- "Select a partner and position in a grid. One student in each pair begins the drill with a ball and the other defends."
- "The attacker tries to maintain possession from the defender for 10 seconds. Players must stay in the confines of the grid."
- "I will signal the start and end of each 10-second period. Repeat the drill 10 times with a short rest between each repetition. Then partners will switch roles and repeat the drill 10 more times."
- "The attacker receives 1 point whenever he or she maintains possession within the grid for 10 seconds. The defender receives 1 point if he or she tackles the ball before 10 seconds has elapsed. Each player can score 10 points as attacker and 10 points as defender. Keep track of your points when attacking and defending."

Student Options

- "Creatively combine shielding and dribbling skills to elude the defender and maintain ball possession."
- "The defender may use either block or poke tackles to win possession."

Student Keys to Success

Attacker

- Position sideways between the defender and ball and control ball with foot farthest from the defender.
- Quickly change speed and direction.
- Use deceptive body feints to unbalance the defender.

Defender

- Use tight marking.
- Focus vision on the ball.
- Anticipate movements of attacker.
- Tackle the ball at opportune moment.

Student Success Goals

- 6 points or more scored when attacking
- 6 points or more scored when defending

To Decrease Difficulty

- Tell players to execute the drill at half speed.
- Reduce the Success Goal.

To Increase Difficulty

- Increase drill time from 10 to 15 seconds.
- Decrease grid size to restrict maneuvering.
- Increase the Success Goal.

2. *Receive Under Pressure*
[Corresponds to *Soccer*, Step 5, Drill 2]

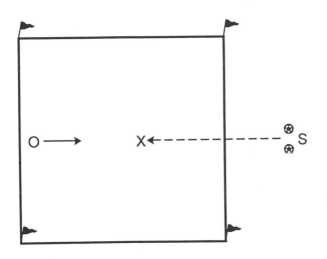

Group Management and Safety Tips

- Use cones or flags to outline a 10-by-10-yard area for each group of three students.
- Keep at least 5 yards between grids.
- Caution students to watch out for classmates in other grids when retrieving stray balls.

Equipment

- 1 or 2 balls per group of three students
- Cones, flags, or other markers to outline areas

Instructions to Class

- "Divide into groups of three. Designate one player as server, one as defender and one as attacker. Position within a grid."
- "The server should stand 15 yards from the grid with the soccer ball or balls. The attacker stands in the center of the grid facing the server and the defender stands 5 yards behind the attacker, near the edge of the grid."
- "On my command the server passes to the attacker who must control and protect the ball from the defender. Both attacker and defender must stay in the grid."
- "The attacker receives 1 point for maintaining possession for 10 seconds. The defender receives 1 point for gaining possession in fewer than 10 seconds."
- "Repeat the drill 10 times, switch roles, and repeat again. I will signal the beginning and end of each 10-second repetition."
- "We will continue until all group members have played 10 repetitions in each role."

Student Option

- ''The server may serve ground or lofted balls to the attacker.''

Student Keys to Success

Attacker

- Move toward the ball to receive and control it.
- Position to shield the ball from the defender.
- Change direction suddenly to unbalance defender.

Defender

- Maintain balance and body control.
- Anticipate attacker movements.

- Focus vision on the ball.
- Do not slide tackle.
- Tackle at opportune moment.

Student Success Goals

- 7 or more points scored when attacker
- 7 or more points scored when defender

To Decrease Difficulty

- Position server 5 yards from attacker.
- Shorten the drill to 5 seconds.
- Decrease the Success Goal.

To Increase Difficulty

- Require server to loft passes.
- Allow defender to start by standing directly behind attacker.
- Increase the Success Goal.

3. Receive and Turn

[Corresponds to *Soccer*, Step 5, Drill 3]

Group Management and Safety Tips

- Same as Drill 2.

Equipment

- Same as Drill 2.

Instructions to Class

- ''This drill is a natural extension of Drill 2 and is set up the same. In this drill, though, to score 1 point the attacker must not only maintain possession of the ball within the grid but also turn and face the defender.''
- ''Each repetition of the drill will last 10 seconds. The defender receives 1 point if he or she prevents the attacker from turning with the ball within the grid.''
- ''I will signal the beginning and end of each 10-second repetition. We will continue until each student has played 10 repetitions in each role.''

Student Option

- ''The server may pass ground or lofted balls to the attacker.''

Student Keys to Success

Attacker

- Move to the ball to receive it.
- Shield the ball from the defender.
- Change direction suddenly to unbalance the defender.
- Create space in which to turn with the ball.
- Quickly turn and face defender.

Defender

- Maintain good balance and body control.
- Anticipate attacker movements.
- Focus vision on ball.
- Tightly mark attacker.
- Tackle the ball if attacker tries to turn.

Student Success Goals

- 5 or more points scored when attacker
- 8 or more points scored when defender

To Decrease Difficulty

- Position the server 5 yards from the attacker.
- Shorten the drill 5 seconds.
- Decrease the Success Goal.

To Increase Difficulty

- Require the server to loft all passes.
- Position the defender directly behind the attacker.
- Increase the Success Goal.

4. Receive, Turn and Dribble
[Corresponds to *Soccer*, Step 5, Drill 4]

Group Management and Safety Tips

- Same as Drill 2.

Equipment

- Same as Drill 2.

Instructions to Class

- "This drill emphasizes another principle of individual attack: dribbling at the defender. This drill is a natural extension of Drills 2 and 3 and is set up the same as Drill 2."
- "The attacker receives 1 point for turning with the ball and 1 additional point for dribbling and beating the defender in the grid. As before, the drill lasts 10 seconds."
- "The defender receives 2 points for preventing the attacker from turning with the ball."
- "Each group member will play 10 repetitions in each role. I will signal the beginning and end of each 10-second period."

Student Option

- "The server may pass ground or lofted balls to the attacker."

Student Keys to Success

Attacker

- Move to the ball to receive it.
- Shield the ball from defender.

- Change direction suddenly to unbalance the defender.
- Create space before turning with ball.
- Turn and dribble at defender.

Defender

- Maintain good balance and body control.
- Anticipate the movements of attacker.
- Focus vision on the ball.
- Tightly mark attacker.
- Force attacker to dribble laterally.

Student Success Goals

- 12 or more points scored as attacker
- 12 or more points scored as defender

To Decrease Difficulty

- Increase grid size.
- Decrease the Success Goal.

To Increase Difficulty

- Require server to loft all serves.
- Permit the defender to stand directly behind the attacker.
- Increase the Success Goal.

5. *One Versus One to a Central Goal*

[Corresponds to *Soccer*, Step 5, Drill 5]

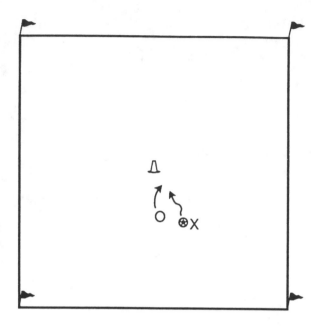

Group Management and Safety Tips

- Use flags or cones to outline a 15-by-15-yard grid for each pair of students. Place a single cone in the center of each grid.
- Keep at least 5 yards between grids.
- Place a couple extra balls near each grid so students do not waste time chasing stray balls.
- Caution students to watch for classmates in other grids if retrieving a stray ball.

Equipment

- 1 ball per student pair
- Cones, flags, or other markers to outline the playing area and designate the central goal

Instructions to Class

- "Select a partner and position in a grid."
- "Partners play one versus one against each other in the grid. The drill consists of two 5-minute periods with a short rest between periods. Each student will be attacker for one 5-minute period and defender for the other."
- "The attacker receives 1 point for beating the defender on the dribble and 1 point for passing the ball and hitting the central goal (cone). The defender receives 1 point for successfully tackling and gaining possession of the ball. If the defender steals the ball he or she immediately returns it to the attacker and they continue the drill."
- "I will signal the beginning and end of each 5-minute period. Total your points scored as an attacker and a defender."

Student Option

- None

Student Key to Success

- Use correct decision making.

Student Success Goals

- More points scored than partner when attacker
- More points scored than partner when defender

To Decrease Difficulty

- Shorten playing time to 2-minute periods.

To Increase Difficulty

- Enlarge playing area.
- Increase playing time to 7-minute periods.
- Position two goals in the grid area.

6. Defend the Line
[Corresponds to *Soccer*, Step 5, Drill 6]

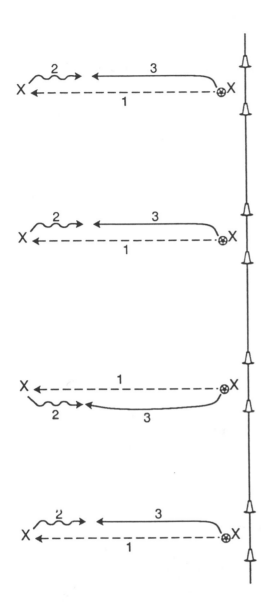

Instructions to Class

- ''Pair with a classmate and decide which of you will be the attacker and which the defender. Each group should position near one of the goals marked on the sideline (endline) of the field.''
- ''The defender stands between the cones with a soccer ball and the attacker stands 25 yards away, facing the defender.''
- ''The defender serves the ball to the attacker, who controls and dribbles it toward goal. The defender closes on and challenges the attacker. The attacker receives 1 point for dribbling past the defender and through the goal. The defender receives 1 point for tackling and gaining possession of the ball.''
- ''Repeat the drill 20 times, then switch roles and repeat 20 more times. Keep track of the points you score when attacking and when defending.''

Student Option

- ''The defender may serve ground or lofted balls to the attacker.''

Student Keys to Success

Attacker

- Receive and control the ball with as few touches as possible.
- Use deceptive body feints to unbalance the defender.
- Beat the defender on the dribble.

Defender

- Immediately close the distance to the attacker.
- Maintain balance and body control.
- Anticipate the attacker's movements.
- Focus vision on the ball.
- Force the attacker to dribble laterally across the field.
- Tackle the ball at an opportune moment.

Group Management and Safety Tips

- Along a field's endlines or sidelines position two cones or flags to represent a goal 8 yards wide for each pair of students.
- Position goals at least 15 yards apart.

Equipment

- 1 ball per two students
- Cones, flags, or similar markers

Student Success Goals

- More points scored than partner as attacker
- More points scored than partner as defender

To Decrease Difficulty

- Start attacker 15 yards from defender.
- Require defender to serve ground balls.

To Increase Difficulty for Attacker

- Decrease the goal width so the attacker must beat the defender in a narrower lane.
- Require the attacker to control each serve with two or fewer touches.

To Increase Difficulty for Defender

- Increase the goal width to 12 yards so the defender must protect a greater area.

7. *One Versus One With Two Goals*

[Corresponds to *Soccer*, Step 5, Drill 7]

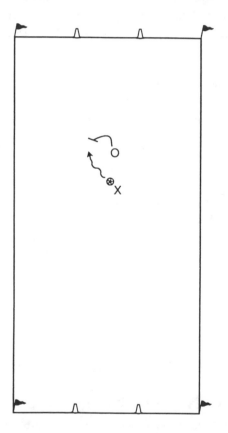

Instructions to Class

- ''This simulated game situation incorporates all of the individual tactics of attack and defense. Pair up with a classmate and position in one of the grids. Play one versus one against your classmate within the grid. One player starts with the ball.''
- ''You receive 1 point each time you pass the ball through the opponent's goal. Change of possession occurs after each point scored. The first player to score 10 points wins.''

Student Option

- ''If extra cones are available, you may place two small goals on each endline of the grid.''

Student Keys to Success

- Use the individual tactics of attack and defense.
- Make appropriate decisions for each situation.

Student Success Goal

- 10 points scored before your opponent

To Decrease Difficulty

- Play to 5 points.

To Increase Difficulty

- Play to 15 points.

Group Management and Safety Tips

- Outline a 10-by-20-yard area for each student pair. Use cones or flags to designate a small goal on each 10-yard endline.
- Keep at least 5 yards between playing grids.

Equipment

- 1 ball per student pair
- Cones, flags, or other markers

8. One-On-One Team Game
[New Drill]

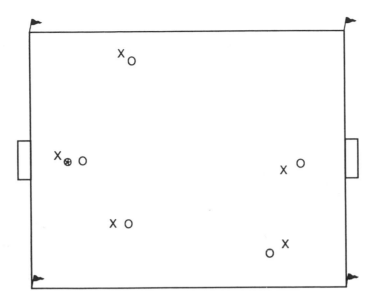

Group Management and Safety Tips

- Use cones, flags, or similar markers to out-line a 40-by-50-yard area for each game. Position a regulation goal on each endline. If portable goals are unavailable, use cones or flags for goalposts.
- Divide class into equal teams of 5 to 7 players.
- Do not use goalkeepers.

Equipment

- Cones, flags, or similar markers
- Colored scrimmage vests to differentiate teams
- Portable goals
- 1 ball per game

Instructions to Class

- ''Two teams play on a field. Each team defends one goal and tries to score in the opponent's goal.''
- ''Begin the game with a kickoff from the center of the field. Follow regular soccer rules except the offside rule. Because goals can be scored from any distance and neither team has a goalkeeper, defending players must use tight one-on-one cover-age to protect their goal. Each player must mark a specific opponent.''
- ''Play for 20 minutes. The team that scores the most goals wins.''

Student Option

- None

Student Keys to Success

- Use tight marking.
- Position goalside of opponent.
- Keep ball and opponent being marked in vision.
- Maintain balance and body control.
- React to opponent movements.
- Don't be fooled by body feints or decep-tive movements.

Student Success Goal

- Prevent the opponent you are marking from scoring.

To Decrease Difficulty

- Shorten the drill to reduce its physical demands.
- Decrease the size of the goals to make defense easier.

To Increase Difficulty

- Lengthen the drill to increase its physical demands.
- Use two balls instead of one.
- Add two additional goals to make defense more difficult.

Step 6 Heading Skills

Soccer is the only game in which players literally use their heads to propel the ball. Heading skills can be used to pass the ball, to score goals, and for defensive clearances around the goal. Successful headers combine proper technique, courage, and determination to outjump opponents who are also trying to head the ball.

Two heading techniques are generally used in game competition. The jump header is useful in many situations whereas the dive header is appropriate only for situations like scoring off of a low cross in the goal mouth. Make sure your students can execute both heading techniques, but caution them never to use the dive header when other players are nearby to avoid being accidentally kicked in the face.

Some beginning students are afraid to head the ball. You can help them overcome their fear by explaining that, if done correctly, heading the ball doesn't hurt at all. To prove your point have each student hold a ball at arm's length, softly toss it and head it off the forehead and back into the hands. Students should repeat the exercise, throwing the ball progressively higher until everyone is comfortably with a ball contacting the head.

Teach students to keep their eyes open and mouths closed when heading the ball. With eyes open they can focus on the ball until the moment it contacts the forehead. With mouths closed they will avoid biting their tongues should they collide with another player.

Jump Header Rating

BEGINNING LEVEL	ADVANCED LEVEL
Preparation	
• Body turned sideways to oncoming ball	• Shoulders square to oncoming ball
• Legs straight, arms tight to sides	• Legs flexed at knee, arms drawn back in preparation to jump up
• Focuses vision on field or opponent rather than on ball	• Head steady with vision focused on ball
Execution	
• Jumps forward	• Jumps up
• Little upward momentum	• Arms thrust upward to generate momentum
• Upper trunk straight	• Upper trunk arched backward from vertical
• Chin up	• Head steady, neck stiff, and chin tucked
• Eyes closed	• Eyes open with focus on ball
• Contacts ball on top of head	• Contacts ball on flat surface of forehead

(Cont.)

BEGINNING LEVEL	ADVANCED LEVEL
Follow-Through • Weak forward snap of upper body • Lands off-balance on ground	• Upper body snaps forward through point of contact • Lands with both feet on ground

Dive Header Rating

BEGINNING LEVEL	ADVANCED LEVEL
Preparation • Body sideways to oncoming ball • Stands upright—little or no crouch	• Shoulders square to oncoming ball • Slightly crouched with knees flexed
Execution • Body is not parallel to ground • Vision focused on ground • Arms at sides • Leads with top of head • Contacts ball on top of head	• Dives forward with body parallel to ground • Head tilted back with vision focused on ball • Arms extended back and down • Head tilted back • Contacts ball on forehead
Follow-Through • Little forward momentum • Hits ground hard	• Propels body forward through point of contact with ball • Arms and hands used to break fall

Error Detection and Correction for Heading Skills

Most heading errors are due to incorrect technique, poor timing, or both. Beginners often have difficulty incorporating all elements of the skill, particularly the timing of the jump. When observing a student executing the jump header, focus your attention on the body position. Shoulders should be square to the ball, eyes open, and mouth closed. The student should jump early, hang in the air for an instant, and then contact the ball on the flat surface of the forehead.

When observing a student execute the dive header, pay particular attention to the head position. The head should be tilted back and firmly positioned so that the ball is headed off the forehead, not the top of the head.

ERROR   **CORRECTION**

Jump Header

1. Student contacts the ball before the highest point of the jump.

1. Emphasize that the timing of the takeoff is critical. Beginning students tend to jump too late and as a result contact the ball before the highest point of the jump. Tell students to jump early, hang in the air for an instant, and then snap forward from the waist and contact the ball with the forehead.

2. Ball is headed weakly.

2. Lack of power usually results from either a weak snap of the upper trunk toward the ball or a weakly positioned head and neck at ball contact. Encourage students to hold the arched position until the last possible moment, then snap forward with power to strike the ball.

3. Student heads the ball inaccurately.

3. Poor accuracy usually results from making improper contact. Tell the student to keep the neck firm and contact the ball on the flat surface of the forehead. Generally, the student should not head the ball off the top or side of the head.

Dive Header

1. The student heads the ball off target.

1. Tell the student to keep the head steady and contact the ball on the flat surface of the forehead. It is essential to focus vision on the ball until the instant of contact with the forehead.

2. The ball pops up off the student's head.

2. This error occurs because the student dips the head just before heading the ball. The student must keep the head steady with the forehead perpendicular to the ground at the moment of ball impact.

Heading Drills

1. *Head Ball to Hands*
[Corresponds to *Soccer*, Step 6, Drill 1]

Group Management and Safety Tips

- Students should stand at least 2 yards apart.
- Students should wear glasses only with unbreakable lenses; students who wear glasses should have a strap to hold them on.

Equipment

- 1 ball per student

Instructions to Class

- ''Everyone get a ball and spread out around the gymnasium (or field). First you must get accustomed to feeling the ball rebounding off your forehead.''
- ''With both hands hold the ball about 18 inches in front of your face. Softly toss the ball off your forehead and nod it back into your hands. Keep your eyes open, mouth closed, and neck stiff at contact.''
- ''Repeat 30 times.''

Student Option

- ''Increase the toss distance as you become more confident.''

Student Keys to Success

- Keep eyes open and vision on ball.
- Keep chin tucked and neck firm.
- Contact ball on forehead.
- Snap upper trunk forward to meet ball.

Student Success Goal

- 30 tosses headed directly back into hands

To Decrease Difficulty

- Head ball directly out of hands.
- Lower the Success Goal.

To Increase Difficulty

- Have students head a ball tossed by a classmate.

2. *Heading From Knees*
[Corresponds to *Soccer*, Step 6, Drill 2]

Group Management and Safety Tips

- Position student pairs at least 3 yards apart.
- Students should wear glasses only with unbreakable lenses and use a strap to hold them in place.

Equipment

- 1 ball per student pair

Instructions to Class

- ''Divide into pairs and face your partner at 2 yards. One partner kneels, the other stands holding a ball. The standing partner will serve.''
- ''The server tosses the ball toward the kneeling player's head. The kneeling player arches his or her upper body backward prior to the serve, then snaps forward from the waist to head the ball back toward the server's chest. The server catches the ball and tosses it again.''
- ''Repeat the drill 30 times, then switch roles and repeat 30 more times.''
- ''Keep your eyes open, mouth closed, and neck firm as you snap forward to head the ball.''

Student Option

- ''The server can vary the distance of the ball toss.''

Student Keys to Success

- Focus vision on ball.
- Arch upper trunk backward in preparation.
- Snap upper trunk forward and contact ball on forehead.
- Keep eyes open and mouth closed.
- Tuck chin, keep neck stiff and head firmly positioned.

Student Success Goal

- 27 of 30 tosses headed to server's chest

To Decrease Difficulty

- Decrease the distance between partners to 1 yard.
- Decrease the Success Goal.

To Increase Difficulty

- Increase the distance between partners.
- Increase the repetitions.
- Increase the speed of repetition.
- Increase the Success Goal.

3. *Jump and Head Stationary Ball*

[Corresponds to *Soccer*, Step 6, Drill 3]

Group Management and Safety Tips

- Separate student pairs by at least 3 yards.
- Students should wear glasses only with unbreakable lenses and use a strap to hold them on.
- Caution students not to jump into the player holding the ball.
- Have students self-pace the drill.

Equipment

- 1 ball per student pair

Instructions to Class

- ''Choose a partner and stand facing him or her at about 2 feet.''
- ''One partner holds a ball in front of and above him or her. The other practices the jump-header technique on the stationary ball. The heading student should jump vertically, arch the upper body backward, snap forward, and head the ball with the flat surface of the forehead.''
- ''The partner should hold the ball tightly so it is not knocked loose. Execute 30 jump headers each.''

Student Option

- ''Partners may stand farther apart so the heading player can step forward before jumping.''

Student Keys to Success

- Use a two-footed takeoff to jump up.
- Arch upper body backward while in the air.
- Snap upper body forward and contact ball on forehead.
- Keep eyes open and mouth closed.
- Touch both feet to ground simultaneously for balance.

Student Success Goal

- 25 of 30 balls contacted on forehead

To Decrease Difficulty

- Require players to jump only a few inches off the ground.
- Reduce the repetitions.
- Lower the Success Goal.

To Increase Difficulty

- Require students to jump as high as possible to head the ball.
- Increase the repetitions.
- Increase the speed of repetition.
- Increase the Success Goal.

4. *Jump Header to Partner*
[Corresponds to *Soccer*, Step 6, Drill 4]

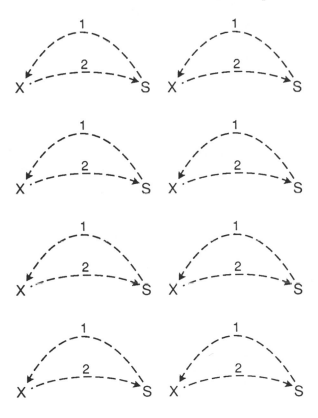

Instructions to Class

- "Stand facing a partner at about 5 yards. One partner serves while the other practices jump-header technique."
- "The server tosses the ball about 12 inches above the partner's head. The partner jumps vertically and heads the ball back to the server's chest. Contact the ball at the highest point of the jump."
- "Execute 20 headers, then switch roles and repeat."

Student Option

- "Vary toss distance and trajectory."

Student Keys to Success

- Square shoulders to the server.
- Use two-footed takeoff to jump up.
- Arch upper trunk backward.
- Snap upper body forward and strike ball with forehead.
- Keep eyes open and mouth closed.

Student Success Goal

- 17 of 20 tosses headed directly to the server's chest

To Decrease Difficulty

- Move partners closer.
- Allow students to head without jumping off the ground.
- Lower the Success Goal.

To Increase Difficulty

- Increase distance between partners.
- Increase the speed of repetition.
- Increase the Success Goal.

Group Management and Safety Tips

- Separate student pairs by at least 3 yards.
- Students should wear glasses only with unbreakable lenses and use a strap to hold them on.
- Have students self-pace the drill.

Equipment

- 1 ball per student pair

5. *Moving Headers*
[Corresponds to *Soccer*, Step 6, Drill 5]

Group Management and Safety Tips
- Separate student pairs by at least 3 yards.
- Students should wear glasses only with unbreakable lenses and use a strap to hold them on.
- Have students self-pace the drill.

Equipment
- 1 ball per student pair

Instructions to Class
- ''This drill is similar to Drill 4 except you will practice jump header technique while moving forward.''
- ''Find a partner and face your partner at about 3 yards. One partner serves while the other practices the jump header.''
- ''The server jogs slowly backward and then tosses the ball toward his or her partner. The partner moves toward the lofted ball, jumps up, and heads it back to the server. Both players jog at the same speed, maintaining 3 yards between them.''
- ''Repeat for 20 tosses, then switch positions and repeat for 20 more.''

Student Options
- ''The server may toss at varying heights and trajectories.''
- ''Partners can begin by walking rather than jogging, then gradually increase speed.''

Student Keys to Success
- Use a two-footed takeoff to jump up.
- Arch upper body backward.
- Focus vision on ball.
- Tuck chin and keep neck stiff.
- Snap upper trunk forward and contact ball on forehead.
- Land on both feet for balance.

Student Success Goal
- 15 of 20 tosses headed to server's chest

To Decrease Difficulty
- Move partners closer.
- Have players walk instead of jog.
- Decrease the Success Goal.

To Increase Difficulty
- Increase distance between partners.
- Increase the speed of repetition.
- Increase the Success Goal.

6. *Head, Catch, and Throw*
[Corresponds to *Soccer*, Step 6, Drill 6]

Group Management and Safety Tips
- Organize players into groups of 3.
- Position groups 10 yards apart or, if space is limited, somewhat closer.
- Students should wear glasses only with unbreakable lenses and use a strap to hold them on.
- Have students self-pace the drill.

Equipment
- 1 ball per group of 3 players

Instructions to Class
- ''Form a triangle with two classmates, keeping 10 yards between players. Number yourselves 1, 2, and 3. Player 1 has the ball.''
- ''Player 1 tosses the ball to 2 who jumps and heads it to 3. Player 3 catches the ball and tosses it to 1 who jumps and heads it to 2. Player 2 catches the ball and tosses to 3 who heads to 1. Continue the throw-head-catch sequence until each player has headed the ball 20 times.''
- ''Self-pace the drill.''

Student Option

- None

Student Keys to Success

- Square shoulders with oncoming ball.
- Use two-footed takeoff to jump up.
- Turn body toward target as upper trunk snaps forward.
- Contact ball on flat surface of forehead.
- Focus vision on ball.

Student Success Goal

- 16 of 20 tosses accurately headed to correct player

To Decrease Difficulty

- Move players closer (smaller triangle).
- Allow players to head without jumping.
- Decrease the Success Goal.

To Increase Difficulty

- Increase distance between players (larger triangle).
- Increase the Success Goal.

7. *Diving Headers*
[Corresponds to *Soccer*, Step 6, Drill 7]

Group Management and Safety Tips

- Conduct this drill on a soft surface: a padded mat indoors or a soft grass surface or sawdust pit outdoors.
- Remind students to use their arms and hands to break their fall.
- Keep at least 5 yards between student pairs.
- Students should wear glasses only with unbreakable lenses and use a strap to hold them on.
- Allow students to self-pace the drill.

Equipment

- 1 ball per student pair

Instructions to Class

- ''Pair up and stand facing your partner at 10 yards. One partner serves while the other practices dive header technique.''
- ''The server tosses the ball at approximately waist height towards his or her partner.''
- ''The header dives parallel to the ground, tilts his or her head back, contacts the ball with the forehead and uses arms and hands to break the fall.''
- ''Head the ball directly back to the server, who shouldn't have to move more than one step in any direction to catch it.''
- ''Execute 10 dive headers, then switch roles and repeat.''

Student Options

- ''When heading you can start from a squat rather than standing position.''
- ''Have the server vary the toss distance.''

Student Keys to Success

- Face the server.
- Flex knees, draw arms back, and spring forward parallel to the ground.
- Keep eyes open and mouth closed.
- Tilt head back and focus on ball.
- Contact ball with forehead.
- Generate enough momentum to continue forward through point of contact.
- Use arms and hands to break fall.

Student Success Goal

- 7 of 10 balls headed accurately to server

To Decrease Difficulty

- Move partners closer.
- Allow the player who is heading the ball to start on all fours.
- Decrease the Success Goal.

To Increase Difficulty

- Players slowly jog before executing the dive header.
- Increase the Success Goal.

8. *Score by Headers Only*
[New Drill]

Group Management and Safety Tips

- Divide the class into two equal teams.
- Play on a full-size field with cones or flags designating a goal 6 yards wide on each endline.
- If a full-size field is not available, reduce team size and play in a proportionately smaller area.

Equipment

- 1 ball per game
- Cones or flags to designate goals
- Colored scrimmage vests to differentiate teams

Instructions to Class

- "I will award one team possession to begin the game. Each team will defend a goal and try to score in the opponent's goal."
- "The team with the ball moves into scoring position by passing (throwing and catching, not kicking) the ball among teammates. A player who receives the ball may take no more than three steps before passing to a teammate. Violation of this rule results in loss of possession to the opposing team."
- "Goals are scored by tossing the ball to a teammate who heads it through the opponent's goal."
- "Neither team has a goalkeeper though all players may intercept passes with their hands. The defending team gains possession by intercepting a pass or recovering a ball dropped or played out-of-bounds by an opponent. Defenders may not wrestle the ball from an opponent."
- "Play for 20 minutes. The team that scores the most goals wins."

Student Option

- "Use either the jump header or dive header to score goals."

Student Keys to Success

- Move the ball upfield with short, precise interpassing, not long high-risk tosses.
- Keep eyes open and mouth closed when heading.
- Head to score on a downward plane toward the goal line.

Team Success Goal

- More goals scored than opponents.

To Decrease Difficulty

- Increase goal size.
- Decrease playing-area size.
- Use four rather than two goals.

To Increase Difficulty

- Decrease goal size.
- Have two balls in play at the same time.
- Increase playing-area size.

Step 7 Shooting Skills

Scoring goals is the most difficult task in soccer. Consistent goal scorers combine shooting skills with intangible qualities such as anticipation, determination, composure under pressure, and courage. Although prolific scorers are rare, through proper training any player can improve his or her scoring ability. You must provide a learning environment that enables students to achieve that objective.

Different shooting techniques are used for rolling, bouncing, or dropping balls. Teach your students the instep drive, full volley, half volley, side volley, and swerve shots. To teach shooting proficiency with either foot, structure shooting drills to alternate use of left and right feet.

Instep Drive Shot Rating

BEGINNING LEVEL	ADVANCED LEVEL
Preparation	
• Plants balance foot behind ball	• Plants balance foot several inches to side of ball
• Keeps balance leg straight	• Balance leg flexed at knee for maximum stability
• Kicking foot flexed rather than extended	• Kicking foot fully extended
• Head unsteady and vision on field or opponent	• Head steady with vision on ball
Execution	
• Shoulders angled to intended target	• Shoulders square with target
• Body behind ball	• Body and knee of kicking leg over ball
• Leans backward as foot contacts ball	• Leans slightly forward as foot contacts ball
• Kicking foot wobbly or uncertain	• Kicking foot firm as it contacts ball
Follow-Through	
• Momentum falls off at point of contact	• Momentum forward through point of contact
• Incomplete follow-through	• Complete follow-through

Full Volley Shot Rating

BEGINNING LEVEL	ADVANCED LEVEL
Preparation	
• Not positioned at spot where ball will drop • Balance leg straight and stiff • Arms tight to side • Head unsteady with vision on opponent or field	• Player moves to spot where ball will drop • Balance leg flexed at knee • Arms out to side for balance • Head steady with vision on ball
Execution	
• Knee of kicking leg behind ball • Player leans backward and reaches with foot to contact ball • Kicking foot uncertain or wobbly • Kicking foot pointed forward and diagonally down at contact • Contacts ball on lower instep near end of the foot	• Knee of kicking leg over ball • Player leans forward as foot contacts ball • Kicking foot firmly positioned • Kicking foot straight downward at contact • Ball contacted on full instep
Follow-Through	
• Momentum falls off at point of contact • Sweeping motion of kicking leg	• Forward momentum through point of contact • Short, powerful snap of leg

Half Volley Shot Rating

BEGINNING LEVEL	ADVANCED LEVEL
Preparation	
• Not positioned at spot where ball will drop • Balance leg straight and stiff • Arms held tight to sides • Head unsteady with vision on opponent or field	• Moves to where ball will drop • Balance leg flexed • Arms extended out from body for balance • Head steady with vision on ball
Execution	
• Knee of kicking leg behind ball • Player leans backward and reaches kicking leg for ball • Kicks ball after it hits and rebounds off of ground • Kicking foot uncertain or wobbly • Kicking foot angled or flexed at contact	• Knee of kicking leg over ball • Player leans forward at contact • Ball kicked at instant it hits ground • Kicking foot firmly positioned • Kicking foot straight downward at contact

(Cont.)

BEGINNING LEVEL	ADVANCED LEVEL
Follow-Through • Momentum falls off at point of contact • Uses sweeping motion of leg	• Forward momentum through point of contact • Short, powerful snap of leg

Side Volley Shot Rating

BEGINNING LEVEL	ADVANCED LEVEL
Preparation • Balance leg straight and stiff • Arms tight to sides • Kicking leg raised to side at angle to ground • Kicking leg straight • Kicking foot somewhat flexed and loose • Head unsteady with vision on field or opponent	• Balance leg flexed at knee • Arms out to sides for balance • Kicking leg raised to side, parallel to ground • Kicking leg flexed with foot drawn back • Kicking foot extended and firmly positioned • Head steady with vision on ball
Execution • Foot contacts center of ball • Kicking foot loosely positioned • Momentum falls short at point of contact	• Instep of foot contacts upper half of ball • Snaplike motion of kicking leg • Body rotates towards ball
Follow-Through • Uses incorrect follow-through • Lacks complete follow-through	• Kicking leg snaps straight • Kick angles diagonally downward through top half of ball

Swerve Shot Rating

BEGINNING LEVEL	ADVANCED LEVEL
Preparation • Balance foot planted behind ball • Balance leg straight and stiff • Kicking foot somewhat flexed • Head unsteady with vision on opponent or field	• Balance foot planted beside ball • Balance leg flexed at knee • Kicking foot fully extended • Head steady with vision on ball

(Cont.)

Swerve Shot Rating (Continued)

BEGINNING LEVEL	ADVANCED LEVEL
Execution • Foot contacts center of ball • Kicking foot loosely positioned • Momentum falls short at point of contact	• Foot contacts ball to left or right of vertical midline • Kicking foot kept firmly positioned • Momentum forward through point of contact
Follow-Through • Uses incorrect follow-through • Follow-through of leg below hips	• Uses inside-out follow-through (motion begins near vertical midline of body and angles outward) for outside-of-the-instep shot, or outside-in follow-through (motion begins to side of vertical midline of body and angles slightly inward toward center, almost across the body) for inside-of-the-instep shot • Follow-through raises kicking foot to waist level or above

Error Detection and Correction for Shooting Skills

Shooting errors generally result from

1. incorrect placement of the balance foot,
2. improper position of the kicking-leg knee in relation to the ball,
3. incorrect position of the kicking foot, or
4. insufficient follow-through motion.

As you observe students in shooting drills or games, watch for these common errors.

 ERROR

 **CORRECTION**

Instep Drive, Full Volley, and Half Volley Shots

1. The ball travels up over the goal.

1. Incorrect position of the balance foot or kicking foot (or both) will cause a shot to travel up over the goal. Tell the student to place the balance foot beside the ball and the kicking-leg knee directly over the ball. The student should not lean back as the ball is struck. The kicking foot should be fully extended and pointed downward as the instep contacts the center of the ball.

ERROR	CORRECTION
2. The shot travels left or right of the goal.	2. Have the student square shoulders and hips with the goal at the instant of the kick. Shoulders at an angle to the target usually cause an inaccurate shot.
3. The shot lacks power.	3. Tell the student to use a complete follow-through to generate maximum power. The student's body weight should transfer forward through the point of contact with the ball.

Side Volley Shot

1. The shot travels up over the goal.	1. The student must kick through the top half of the ball with the instep. Tell the student to raise the kicking leg slightly above ball level, then complete the kicking motion along a downward plane to drive the ball diagonally down.

Swerve Shot

1. The shot fails to swerve in flight.	1. The shooter must impart sufficient spin to the ball to curve the flight trajectory. Have the student contact the ball just left or right of its vertical midline with the outside or inside of the instep. The student must also use an inside-out or outside-in follow-through appropriately.
2. The shot lacks power.	2. Tell the student to contact the ball with as much foot surface as possible and use a complete follow-through.

Shooting Drills

1. Shoot to a Partner
[Corresponds to *Soccer*, Step 7, Drill 2]

Group Management and Safety Tips
- Position groups at least 5 yards apart.
- Have all players shoot in the same direction.

- Have servers roll the ball slowly to the shooter.
- Caution students not to shoot as hard as they can; emphasize accuracy and proper technique over power.

Equipment

- 1 ball per student pair

Instructions to Class

- "Pair up and face a partner at 10 yards. One player serves, the other practices shooting skills."
- "The server rolls the ball toward the shooter, who shoots it back using either the instep drive or swerve shot. Then repeat. Alternate shooting with left and right feet."
- "The shooter receives 1 point for each accurate shot back to the server. Execute 20 instep drive shots and 20 swerve shots, then switch roles and repeat."

Student Option

- "Vary the pace of the serve."

Student Keys to Success

- Square shoulders with target.
- Put knee of kicking leg over ball.

- Keep kicking foot extended and firm.
- Keep head steady with vision on ball.
- Point kicking foot down at moment of contact.
- Contact center of the ball with full instep.
- Use complete follow-through.

Student Success Goals

- 16 of 20 possible points scored with the instep drive
- 14 of 20 possible points scored using the swerve shot

To Decrease Difficulty

- Move partners closer.
- Have the shooter kick a stationary ball to partner.
- Decrease the Success Goal.

To Increase Difficulty

- Move partners farther apart.
- Increase serve velocity.
- Increase the Success Goal.

2. *Shoot Through the Cones*
[Corresponds to *Soccer*, Step 7, Drill 3]

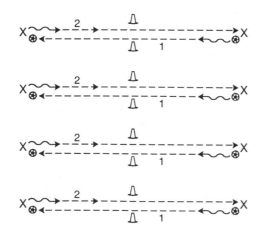

Group Management and Safety Tips

- Separate pairs enough to prevent interference with adjacent groups.
- Use cones, flags, or similar markers to mark a goal 8 yards wide and centered between partners.

Equipment

- 1 ball per student pair
- Cones, flags, or other markers

Instructions to Class

- "Pair with a partner and face each other 50 yards apart on opposite sides of a goal. One partner begins the drill with a ball."
- "The player with the ball dribbles forward a couple of yards and shoots through the goal. The partner collects the ball and tries to score in the same manner from the opposite side. All shots should be taken 20 or more yards from the goal."
- "The shooter receives 1 point for each shot that travels through the cones less than 8 feet off the ground (the height of a regulation goal). Continue until each partner has taken 20 instep drives and 20 swerve shots."
- "Alternate shooting with left and right feet."

Student Option

- "Begin by shooting stationary balls and progress to shooting moving balls."

Student Keys to Success

- Knee of kicking leg positioned over ball at contact.
- Square shoulders with target.
- Kicking foot extends and points down at contact.
- Keep kicking foot firm.
- Keep head steady with vision on ball.
- Use complete follow-through.

Student Success Goals

- 15 or more points scored using the instep drive shot
- 15 or more points scored using the swerve shot

To Decrease Difficulty

- Move players closer to goal.
- Increase goal width.
- Permit players to shoot a stationary ball.
- Reduce the Success Goal.

To Increase Difficulty

- Move players farther from the goal.
- Decrease goal width.
- Increase the Success Goal.

3. Volley Shots to Partner

[Corresponds to *Soccer*, Step 7, Drill 4]

Group Management and Safety Tips

- Position groups 5 yards apart.
- Emphasize correct technique over power.
- Have all players shoot in the same direction.

Equipment

- 1 ball per student pair

Instructions to Class

- "Face a partner at 5 yards. One of you has a ball. The player with the ball drops and volleys it to the partner. The partner catches the ball and returns it in the same manner."
- "Take 10 full volley shots, 10 half volley shots, and 10 side volley shots per partner. You receive 1 point for each volley that is shot directly at your partner's chest so that it could be caught out of the air."
- "Alternate shooting with left and right feet."

Student Options

- "You may position farther from your partner and then step forward before volleying."

- "Vary the serve height as you toss the ball up."

Student Keys to Success

- Square shoulders with target.
- Keep head steady with vision on ball.
- Place knee of kicking leg above the ball at contact with foot.
- Kicking foot firmly positioned upon ball contact.
- Short, powerful snap of kicking leg.

Student Success Goals

- 8 of 10 possible points scored using full volley shot
- 7 of 10 possible points scored using half volley shot
- 6 of 10 possible points scored using side volley shot

To Decrease Difficulty

- Move students closer.
- Reduce the Success Goal.

To Increase Difficulty

- Move students farther apart.
- Require students to volley while jogging.
- Increase the Success Goal.

4. Toss and Volley to Goal
[Corresponds to *Soccer*, Step 7, Drill 5]

Group Management and Safety Tips

- If outdoors, use regulation goals with nets so players need not chase shots on the goal.
- If indoors, use tape to mark off regulation-size goals on the gym wall.
- Several students can share one goal.
- Do not use a goalkeeper.

Equipment

- 1 ball per student
- Goals or similar targets

Instructions to Class

- "Get a soccer ball and position 20 yards in front of a goal. Several students can take turns shooting at the same goal."
- "Toss the ball up so that it will drop a couple of yards in front of you. Move forward and full volley the ball out of the air into the goal. Repeat the drill using half and side volley shots. Execute 10 repetitions of each type of shot."
- "Award yourself 1 point for each shot on goal."
- "Alternate shooting with left and right feet."

Student Option

- "Have a classmate serve the ball."

Student Keys to Success

- Position kicking-leg knee directly above the ball (full and half volley).
- Kick on a downward plane through the ball's top half (side volley).
- Square shoulders with target as ball contacts foot.
- Keep head steady with vision focused on ball.

Student Success Goals

- 7 or more points scored using full volley
- 6 or more points scored using half volley
- 5 or more points scored using side volley

To Decrease Difficulty

- Move the shooter closer to the goal.
- Increase goal size.
- Decrease the Success Goal.

To Increase Difficulty

- Move the shooter farther from the goal.
- Decrease goal size.
- Increase the Success Goal.

5. Control and Shoot
[Corresponds to *Soccer*, Step 7, Drill 6]

Group Management and Safety Tips

- If regular goals are unavailable, use cones or flags to designate a regulation-size goal for each student pair.
- Several student pairs can take turns at one goal.
- Do not use a goalkeeper.

Equipment

- 1 ball per student pair
- Regulation-size goals
- Cones or flags to mark goals

Instructions to Class

- "Pair up. One partner centers 20 yards in front of the goal, the other positions with a ball in the flank area of the field."
- "The flank player serves the ball to the central player, who controls it and shoots to score. The central player tries to control the ball with the first touch and shoot on goal with the second. Award yourself 1 point for each serve you control and score from using only two touches."
- "Repeat 30 times, then partners switch roles and repeat 30 more times."

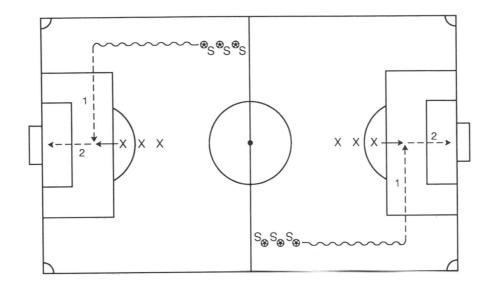

Student Options

- "The flank player may serve ground or lofted balls."
- "Choose the shooting technique."
- "Shoot with either foot."

Student Keys to Success

- Control ball to ground with first touch.
- Square shoulders with target.
- Keep head steady and vision on ball.
- Strike ball on goal with second touch.
- Use complete follow-through.

Student Success Goal

- 15 or more points scored

To Decrease Difficulty

- Move central player closer to the goal.
- Decrease distance between players.
- Require flank player to serve ground balls.
- Allow central player unlimited touches to control and shoot.

To Increase Difficulty

- Move central player farther from the goal.
- Increase distance between players.
- Require flank player to serve lofted balls.
- Increase the Success Goal.

6. Pressure Shooting in the Penalty Area

[Corresponds to *Soccer*, Step 7, Drill 7]

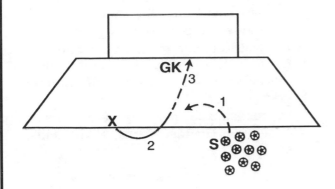

Group Management and Safety Tips

- Students shoot at a regulation-size goal.
- If actual goals are unavailable, use cones or flags to mark several regulation-width goals.
- If indoors, use tape to mark regulation-size goals on the gym wall.

Equipment

- 8 to 10 balls per group
- 1 regulation-size goal per group

Instructions to Class

- "Divide into groups of three. Each group will need 8 to 10 soccer balls."
- "Designate a server, who positions facing the goal at about 25 yards with 8 to 10 balls. A shooter stands with back to the goal, facing the server from 2 yards away. The third player positions in the goal as goalkeeper."
- "The server rolls a ball past the shooter. The shooter quickly turns, sprints to the ball, shoots to score, and sprints back to the original position. The server immediately rolls another ball past the shooter but to the opposite side. The shooter must strike each ball the first time, without setting it up. Continue at maximum speed until the shooter has taken 10 shots at goal. Players then switch roles and repeat."
- "The shooter receives 2 points for each goal scored and 1 point for each shot on goal saved by the goalkeeper."
- "Repeat the drill until each player has taken 10 shots."
- "Alternate shooting with left and right feet."

Student Options

- "The server can roll or bounce balls past the shooter."
- "Choose the shooting technique most appropriate for the type of serve."

Student Keys to Success

- Quickly turn and sprint to ball.
- Square shoulders with target.
- Position kicking-leg knee over ball with foot extended down.
- Keep head steady with vision on ball.
- Use complete follow-through.

Student Success Goal

- 15 or more of 20 possible points scored

To Decrease Difficulty

- Move shooter closer to the goal.
- Decrease the speed of repetition.
- Decrease the number of shots taken (and Success Goal) to reduce the drill's physical demands.
- Decrease the Success Goal.

To Increase Difficulty

- Have the server widely vary the type of serve.
- Increase the repetitions.
- Increase the Success Goal.

7. Game With a Central Goal
[Corresponds to *Soccer*, Step 7, Drill 8]

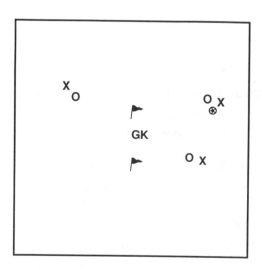

Group Management and Safety Tips

- Use markers to outline a 40-by-40-yard grid for each group of seven students. Place two markers in the center of the grid to represent a goal 8 yards wide.
- Keep at least 5 yards between grids.
- Caution players to watch for others when retrieving a ball that rolls into another grid.
- Instruct goalkeeper to wear suitable equipment (padded pants, elbow pads, etc.).

Equipment

- 1 ball per group of 7 students
- Cones, flags, or similar markers to outline the playing grids and to designate the central goal
- Colored scrimmage vests to differentiate teams

Instructions to Class

- "Divide into groups of seven and position in a 40-by-40-yard grid. Designate one player as a neutral goalkeeeper. Form two teams of three players with the remaining group. One team begins with the ball while the other team defends."
- "The goalkeeper positions between the goalposts to save all shots. Goals can be scored from either side of the goal so the goalkeeper must constantly watch the ball and adjust position accordingly. A shot that travels between the goalposts below the goalkeeper's height counts as a score. A ball that strays from the playing area should be returned by a throw-in. If the defending team wins possession, its players immediately switch to attack while the opponents immediately switch to defense. If the goalkeeper makes a save, he or she throws the ball to an open area in the grid and allow teams to compete for possession."

- "Keep total of goals scored for each team. Play for 15 minutes. I will signal the start and end of play."

Student Options

- "Players call their own fouls, or each group has the goalkeeper act as referee."
- "Choose the shooting technique most appropriate for the situation."

Student Keys to Success

- Work with teammates to create scoring opportunities.
- Move to get free of defenders.
- Look to shoot whenever possible.
- Use correct shooting technique.

Team Success Goal

- More goals scored than opponents.

To Decrease Difficulty

- Enlarge goal size.
- Add a player to the drill who always plays on the team with possession. Thus, the attacking team will always have one more player than the defending team.

To Increase Difficulty

- Reduce goal size.
- Add one player to the drill who always plays on the defending team. Thus, the defending team will always have one more player than the attacking team.

8. Goal Scoring Derby
[Corresponds to *Soccer*, Step 7, Drill 9]

Group Management and Safety Tips

- If outdoors, use the 18-by-44-yard penalty area of a regulation soccer field.
- If indoors, use cones or flags to mark off a similar-sized area and regulation goal for each group of six students.
- Instruct the goalkeeper to wear suitable equipment.

Equipment

- 8 to 10 balls per group
- Cones, flags, or similar markers to outline the field area (if not on a lined soccer field)

- Colored scrimmage vests to differentiate teams

Instructions to Class

- "Divide into groups of six. Designate one player as goalkeeper and one as server; the remaining players form two teams of two."
- "Teams position in the penalty area of the soccer field (or similar area), the goalkeeper positions in the goal, and the server positions at the top of the penalty area with 8 to 10 balls."

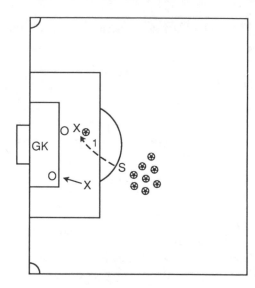

- "The server tosses a ball into the playing area. Teams vie for possession and the team that gains possession tries to score while the other team defends. If a defending player steals the ball, teams switch roles and the new attackers try to score in the common goal. The goalkeeper is neutral and tries to save all shots. If the goalkeeper makes a save, if a goal is scored, or if the ball goes out of the playing area, the server immediately tosses another ball into the area. Continue the drill until the supply of balls runs out."
- "The team scoring the most goals wins. Once the game has finished, designate a new goalkeeper and server, reorganize

the teams, and play again. Repeat the drill until all players have played two versus two."

Student Options

- "The server can vary the type of service."
- "Choose the shooting techniques most appropriate."

Student Keys to Success

- Work with teammate to create scoring opportunities.
- Move to get free of defenders.
- Shoot at every opportunity.
- Use correct shooting technique.

Team Success Goal

- More goals scored than opponents.

To Decrease Difficulty

- Enlarge the goal.
- Add one player to the drill who always plays on the team with possession. Thus, the attacking team will always have a one-player advantage over the defending team.

To Increase Difficulty

- Reduce goal size.
- Add one player to the drill who always plays on the defending team. Thus, the defending team will always have a one-player advantage over the attacking team.

9. *Volley Shooting Game*
[New Drill]

Group Management and Safety Tips

- Use cones, flags, or similar markers to outline a 40-by-50-yard field for each game. Position a regulation-size goal on each endline. If goals are unavailable, use cones or flags to designate goals.
- Divide the class into equal teams of four to six players.
- Do not use goalkeepers.

Equipment

- Cones, flags, or similar markers

- 1 ball per game
- Colored scrimmage vests to differentiate teams

Instructions to Class

- "Two teams position per field; each team defends one goal and attacks an opponent's goal. One team begins the game with possession of the ball."
- "Teams advance the ball through interpassing: throwing and catching the ball. After catching, a player may take only five

steps before passing the ball to a teammate. Players score goals only by volleying a teammate's pass out of the air through the opponent's goal.''

- ''The defending team gains possession if
  1. a defending player intercepts a pass,
  2. the ball goes out of play off an opponent,
  3. an opponent scores,
  4. an opponent drops the ball to the ground, or
  5. an opponent takes more than five steps with the ball.''

- ''Play for 25 minutes. The team that scores the most goals wins.''

Student Option

- ''Use full volley, half volley, or side volley shots to score.''

Student Keys to Success

- Use accurate short range passes to advance ball.
- Keep head steady with vision on ball when preparing to shoot.
- Raise knee over ball to ensure low trajectory on volley shots.

Team Success Goal

- More goals scored than opponents.

To Decrease Difficulty

- Allow students to shoot ball after one bounce.
- Add two more goals to the game.

To Increase Difficulty

- Add goalkeepers.
- Reduce goal size.

10. Long Distance Shooting Game
[New Drill]

Group Management and Safety Tips

- Use cones, flags, or similar markers to outline a 30-by-45-yard area for each game. Set a regulation-size goal on each endline. If goals are unavailable, use cones or flags to designate goalposts.
- Divide the class into teams of four: three field players and one goalkeeper.

Equipment

- Cones, flags, or similar markers
- Colored scrimmage vests to differentiate teams
- 1 ball per game

Instructions to Class

- ''Two teams play on a field; each team defends a goal and attacks an opponent's goal. A goalkeeper guards each goal.''
- ''All shots must be taken 15 yards or more from the goals. Players score 2 points for each goal scored and 1 point for a shot on goal saved by the goalkeeper. Shots that miss count zero. Except for scoring, regular soccer rules apply.''

- ''Play for 20 minutes. Keep total of your team points. The team that scores the most points wins.''

Student Option

- ''Use any shooting technique we have practiced.''

Student Keys to Success

- Use correct shooting technique.
- Keep shots low.
- Shoot at every opportunity.
- Emphasize power and accuracy.

Team Success Goal

- More points scored than opponents.

To Decrease Difficulty

- Allow students to score from any range.
- Increase goal size.
- Do not use goalkeepers.

To Increase Difficulty

- Require shots to be taken from 20 yards or greater.
- Decrease goal size.

Step 8 Goalkeeping

The goalkeeper is the soccer team's one true specialist, who uses entirely different skills than field players. The position is demanding, both mentally and physically, and requires a special player.

Though only one goalkeeper per team plays in actual games, you should familiarize all students with goalkeeping skills to provide them with a greater appreciation for the goalkeeper's difficult role and to prepare them to play in the goal should the situation arise. Goalkeeping skills begin with proper stance—the ready position—and progress to techniques used for receiving balls that are low (rolling), medium high (between ankles and waist), chest high, and high (head height or above). The keeper must also learn to dive to either side to save shots. But saves are only half the goalkeeper's job. He or she must also distribute the ball to teammates by throwing or punting.

Diving is usually the most difficult skill to teach. If you have not been a goalkeeper and are thus unable to adequately demonstrate diving skills, invite an experienced goalkeeper to assist you in teaching diving. Instructional videos may also help. Either way, students will benefit from watching an experienced player demonstrate correct technique.

Goalkeeper Stance Rating

BEGINNING LEVEL	ADVANCED LEVEL
Preparation	
• Remains stationary as ball changes location	• Adjusts properly to movement of ball
• Unprepared for shots on goal	• Anticipates shot as opponent moves into range of goal
• Focuses vision on opponent or field rather than on ball	• Total concentration focused on ball
Execution	
• Shoulders angled to ball	• Shoulders square to ball
• Feet a few inches apart	• Feet shoulder-width apart
• Leans back on heels	• Weight centered evenly over balls of both feet
• Arms and hands at sides	• Hands at waist level with palms forward and fingers pointed up
• Upper body hunched forward	• Upper body erect
• Head unsteady with vision on opponent or field	• Head steady with vision on ball
Follow-Through	
• Reacts slowly to shot	• Reacts instantly to shot

Error Detection and Correction for the Goalkeeper Stance

The goalkeeper should assume the ready position whenever the ball moves into shooting range. This position enables the keeper to quickly react in any direction to make a save.

Observe your students as they practice the ready position to make sure their weight is evenly distributed and they maintain good balance.

ERROR

CORRECTION

ERROR	CORRECTION
1. The goalkeeper leans back on heels.	1. Have the goalkeeper center his or her weight over the balls of both feet with heels slightly elevated off the ground. Feet should position shoulder-width apart with toes pointing toward the ball.

Receiving a Ball Rolling Directly at the Goalkeeper Rating

BEGINNING LEVEL	ADVANCED LEVEL
Preparation • Fails to assume ready position • Feet remain planted as ball changes position • Focuses vision on field or opponent rather than on ball	• Assumes ready position when ball enters shooting range • Adjusts to square shoulders to ball position • Head steady with vision focused on ball
Execution • Spreads legs apart as ball arrives • Bends legs at knees when reaching down for ball • Tries to catch ball with fingers	• Keeps legs close enough that ball cannot skip between • Keeps legs straight when bending to collect ball • Lets ball contact palms then roll up onto wrists and forearms
Follow-Through • Lets ball bounce away • Remains stooped and holds ball in hands	• Curls forearms around ball • Stands erect and clutches ball to chest

Receiving a Ball Rolling to the Side of the Goalkeeper Rating

BEGINNING LEVEL	ADVANCED LEVEL
Preparation	
• Fails to assume ready position	• Assumes ready position when ball enters scoring range
• Keeps feet planted	• Extends lead foot laterally across goal in direction of movement
• Kneels with trailing leg at an angle to goal line	• Kneels with trailing leg parallel to goal line
• Focuses vision on opponent or field rather than on ball	• Keeps head steady with vision on ball
Execution	
• Shoulders angled when kneeling to collect ball	• Keeps shoulders square to oncoming ball
• Heel of lead foot and knee of trailing leg separated	• Heel of lead foot and knee of trailing leg only a few inches apart
• Tries to pin ball to ground with palms	• Palms face forward with fingers pointed down as ball rolls onto wrists and forearms
Follow-Through	
• Tries to hold ball in hands	• Secures ball to chest with forearms

Error Detection and Correction for Receiving Rolling Balls

Errors in receiving rolling balls generally result from improper body and leg position in relation to the ball, trying to catch the ball, or both. Observe as students attempt to receive and control the rolling ball: Beginners often mistakenly try to catch the ball in their hands, much like one would field a ground ball in softball. Remind them that because the soccer ball is much larger than a softball, it cannot be fielded in the same manner.

ERROR | **CORRECTION**

1. The ball skips through the goalkeeper's hands and legs and into the goal.

1. Always have the goalkeeper position between the ball and goal when fielding a ball rolling directly at him or her. Emphasize that he or she should stand with legs close enough that the ball cannot slip between them. When fielding a ball rolling to the side, have the goalkeeper kneel with the lead heel just a few inches from the trailing knee.

2. The goalkeeper tries to catch the ball but it bounces out of control in front of the goal.

2. The goalkeeper should not try to catch a rolling ball, but should allow the ball to roll onto the wrists and forearms. The goalkeeper should then stand and clutch the ball to the chest.

Receiving a Medium-Height Ball Out of the Air Rating

BEGINNING LEVEL	ADVANCED LEVEL
Preparation • Fails to assume ready position • Body out of line with oncoming ball • Positions arms at waist level with palms forward and fingers pointed up	• Assumes ready position when ball enters scoring range • Body between ball and goal • Arms are extended down, fingers pointed down, palms facing forward, and legs slightly apart
Execution • Keeps upper body erect as ball arrives • Dips knees and tries to catch ball in palms	• Bends forward at waist as ball arrives • Keeps legs straight and allows ball to contact wrists then roll onto forearms
Follow-Through • Arms held rigid as ball impacts hard • Ball bounces off hands and out of control	• Jumps slightly backward to cushion impact as ball contacts arms • Clutches ball between forearms and chest

Receiving a Chest-High Ball Rating

BEGINNING LEVEL	ADVANCED LEVEL
Preparation	
• Fails to assume ready position	• Assumes ready position when ball enters range of goal
• Body out of line with oncoming ball	• Shoulders squared to oncoming ball
• Feet a few inches apart	• Feet shoulder-width apart
• Hands extended down or to sides	• Hands extended toward ball in W position
Execution	
• Head to side of hands as ball arrives	• Looks through window formed by thumb and forefingers as ball arrives
• Tries to catch ball in palms	• Receives ball on fingertips
Follow-Through	
• Keeps arms firm at impact	• Withdraws arms and hands to cushion impact
• Ball bounces off hands and out of control	• Secures ball to chest

Receiving a High Ball Rating

BEGINNING LEVEL	ADVANCED LEVEL
Preparation	
• Shoulders at angle to oncoming ball	• Squares shoulders with oncoming ball
• Body out of line with ball	• Body between ball and goal
• Leans back with weight on heels	• Weight centered over balls of feet
• Remains in place	• Moves toward ball in preparation to jump
Execution	
• Uses two-leg takeoff	• Uses one-leg takeoff to jump up
• Arms at shoulder height	• Arms thrust above head
• Hands far apart	• Hands in W position with thumbs and forefingers almost touching
• Head and hands out of line with ball trajectory	• Head and hands in line with oncoming ball
• Arms extended too late	• Catches ball on fingertips and palms at highest point of jump
Follow-Through	
• Arms and hands remain solidly positioned at ball impact	• Arms withdrawn toward body to cushion impact
• Off balance landing	• Lands on both feet with good balance

Error Detection and Correction for Receiving Balls Out of the Air

Errors usually occur because the student fails to position between the ball and the goal, position hands properly, catch the ball at the highest point of the jump, or a combination of these. Pay particular attention to these key aspects of performance when students receive medium-high, chest-high, and high balls.

ERROR   **CORRECTION**

Medium-High Ball

1. Goalkeeper tries to catch the ball with the palms but fails to hold it.

1. Catching a hard shot with the palms is very difficult. Tell the student to extend the arms and hands downward with palms forward, then let the ball contact the wrists and roll up onto the forearms. Only then can the student clutch it to the chest.

2. The ball rebounds off the goalkeeper's hands.

2. Emphasize cushioning the ball impact, especially for a hard shot. Instruct the goalkeeper to do so by jumping back a few inches at ball arrival.

Chest-High Ball

1. Ball slips through the goalkeeper's hands.

1. This error usually occurs because the hands are too far apart. The goalkeeper should receive the ball with the hands in the W position with the thumbs and forefingers almost touching behind the ball. Also tell the goalkeeper to always position between the ball and goal, just in case the ball slips between the hands.

High Ball

1. The goalkeeper fails to catch the ball at the highest possible point.

1. Timing the jump is very important. Have the goalkeeper use a one-footed takeoff to jump up and thrust both arms simultaneously upward to generate momentum. Instruct the goalkeeper to receive the ball by reaching up and catching it at the highest possible point.

Diving to Save Rating

BEGINNING LEVEL	ADVANCED LEVEL
Preparation	
• Fails to assume ready position	• Assumes ready position as ball enters shooting range of goal
• Remains stationary as ball changes location	• Shuffles across goal mouth to position between ball and goal
Execution	
• Steps in wrong direction before dive	• Steps in direction of dive with foot nearest ball
• Vaults forward when diving	• Pushes off with foot nearest ball and vaults sideways to intercept
• Dives on stomach or back	• Dives on side with arms extended toward ball
• Misses or fumbles ball	• Catches ball with fingers and palms
Follow-Through	
• Fails to pin the ball to ground	• Pins ball to ground with extended arms, one hand on top and one behind ball
• Keeps arms extended	• Pulls ball to chest

Error Detection and Correction for Diving to Save

Diving is difficult to master, partly because it is difficult to practice, especially on hard or uneven surfaces. To avoid bumps and bruises always practice diving skills on a soft surface such as a gymnasium mat, outdoor sawdust pit, or soft grass field. Most diving errors occur because the student fails to vault sideways toward the ball, fails to dive on his or her side, fails to pin the ball to the ground, or a combination of these.

ERROR ⊘

CORRECTION

1. The ball bounces out of the goalkeeper's grasp.

1. The goalkeeper cannot afford to mishandle the ball in the goal area. If not absolutely sure of a catch he or she should use the lower hand's open palm to deflect the ball wide of the goal.

ERROR   **CORRECTION**

2. The goalkeeper dives on the stomach.	2. For safety, insist that goalkeepers dive on their sides. Tell them to take a step in the direction of the ball, push off with the foot nearest the ball, vault sideways, and land on one side, with extended arms pinning the ball to the ground.

Distribution by Rolling the Ball Rating

BEGINNING LEVEL	ADVANCED LEVEL
Preparation • Shoulders angled to intended target • Holds ball with fingers and palm	• Squares shoulders with target • Cups ball between palm and wrist
Execution • Stands very erect with knees straight • Releases ball several inches above ground • Ball bounces toward target	• Bends forward at waist and steps toward target with foot opposite ball • Draws back throwing arm and releases ball at ground level with bowling-type motion • Ball rolls toward target
Follow-Through • Arm stops motion at release • Weight stationary over feet	• Throwing arm extends toward target in follow-through • Weight moves toward target

Distribution by Baseball Throw Rating

BEGINNING LEVEL	ADVANCED LEVEL
Preparation • At angle to target • Ball held too far forward	• Faces target • Ball held behind ear in palm

(Cont.)

Distribution by Baseball Throw Rating (Continued)

BEGINNING LEVEL	ADVANCED LEVEL
Execution	
• Keeps feet together or steps away from target • Pushes ball • Throws ball above teammate's feet	• Steps toward target with foot opposite ball • Uses three-quarter or overhand motion and snaps wrist toward target for velocity and distance • Throws ball to teammate's feet
Follow-Through	
• Throwing arm stops after release • Weight stationary over feet	• Uses complete follow-through • Weight moves toward target

Distribution by the Javelin Throw Rating

BEGINNING LEVEL	ADVANCED LEVEL
Preparation	
• Holds ball in palm • Keeps upper body erect prior to throw • Flexes throwing arm at elbow	• Encases ball in fingers, palm, and wrist • Arches upper body back and extends throwing arm • Keeps throwing arm straight
Execution	
• Keeps feet together or steps away from target • Throws ball with arm action only • Throw follows high-lofted arc • Throws ball above teammate's feet	• Steps toward target with foot opposite ball • Uses whiplike motion of arm followed by transfer of weight toward target • Ball follows slightly upward trajectory • Throws ball to teammate's feet
Follow-Through	
• Arm stops after release • Weight stationary over feet	• Uses complete follow-through • Weight transfers toward target

Distribution by Punting the Ball Rating

BEGINNING LEVEL	ADVANCED LEVEL
Preparation • Body angled to target • Extends arms forward and holds ball at knee height • Vision on field or opponent rather than on ball	• Faces target • Extends arms forward and holds ball at waist level in hand opposite kicking foot • Head steady with vision on ball
Execution • Keeps feet together or steps away from target • Kicking foot somewhat flexed • Contacts ball on front portion of instep	• Steps toward target with nonkicking foot • Draws back kicking leg with foot fully extended and firmly positioned • Contacts center of ball with central area of instep
Follow-Through • Nonkicking foot remains planted • Kicking leg stops at contact	• Nonkicking foot leaves ground due to momentum of kicking leg swinging up • Kicking leg reaches waist level or higher on follow-through

Error Detection and Correction for Goalkeeper Distribution

Accuracy is paramount for distributing the ball. Distance is secondarily important. Goalkeepers must also distribute the ball so that teammates can control it with their feet. As you evaluate students, focus your comments on these aspects of performance.

ERROR    **CORRECTION**

Distribution by Rolling or Throwing

1. The ball bounces toward the target.

1. This occurs when the goalkeeper releases the ball above ground level. Have the student use a bowling-type motion to release the ball at ground level.

ERROR 🚫

CORRECTION

2. The goalkeeper's baseball or javelin throws lack accuracy.

2. Have the goalkeeper face the target, step toward it, and completely follow through with the throwing arm. The goalkeeper's weight should transfer toward the target when releasing the ball.

3. The throw lacks distance.

3. In the baseball throw, the goalkeeper must snap the wrist toward the target at ball release. This wrist action imparts velocity and distance. In the javelin throw, the goalkeeper must fully extend his or her throwing arm back with the ball encased between the fingers, palm, and wrist. A powerful whiplike motion of the throwing arm propels the ball over a great distance.

Distribution by Punting

1. The punt lacks accuracy.

1. Have the goalkeeper square shoulders with the target at contact. This prevents the punt from pulling to the right or left of the target.

2. The punt lacks distance.

2. Proper ball release and a complete kicking-leg follow-through send the ball over a long distance. Have the goalkeeper hold the ball at about waist level with the hand opposite the kicking leg, then step forward with the nonkicking foot and punt the ball. The goalkeeper must not release the ball too soon, but just prior to contact with the instep. Tell the goalkeeper to kick through the point of contact so that the kicking foot follows through to chest level or higher.

Goalkeeper Drills

1. *Bounce and Catch*
[Corresponds to *Soccer*, Step 8, Drill 1]

Group Management and Safety Tips
- Conduct this drill on a hard surface.
- Position students at least 2 yards apart.
- Allow students to self-pace the drill.

Equipment
- 1 ball per student

Instructions to Class
- "Goalkeepers must learn to catch with hands in the W position. Everyone get a ball and hold it with both hands at chest level. Bounce the ball hard off the ground, then catch it as it rebounds. Make sure your hands are in the W position and receive the ball on your fingertips."
- "Catch the ball before it passes waist level. Repeat 40 times."

Student Option
- "Execute the drill either from a stationary position or while slowly jogging."

Student Keys to Success
- Keep hands in W position.
- Focus vision on ball.
- Catch ball on fingertips.
- Cushion impact by withdrawing hands on contact.

Student Success Goal
- 36 of 40 balls caught and held with hands in W position

To Decrease Difficulty
- Have students bounce the ball softer off the ground.
- Decrease the Success Goal.

To Increase Difficulty
- Have players bounce the ball very hard off the ground and catch it before it passes thigh level.
- Increase the Success Goal.

2. *Jump and Catch*
[Corresponds to *Soccer*, Step 8, Drill 2]

Group Management and Safety Tips
- Have all players jog in the same direction.
- Keep players at least 3 yards apart so they can safely move sideways to catch the ball.

Equipment
- 1 ball per student

Instructions to Class
- "Everyone get a ball and position along the field endline. Slowly jog forward, toss the ball up high, and jump up with a one-footed takeoff. Extend your arms and hands to catch the ball at the highest point of your jump."
- "Jog in a straight line to avoid colliding."
- "Repeat 30 times."

Student Option
- "Vary the toss height."

Student Keys to Success
- Jump up with a one-footed takeoff.
- Thrust arms upward for additional momentum.
- Focus vision on the ball.
- Catch ball at highest point of jump with hands in the W position.

Student Success Goal

- 25 of 30 balls caught at highest point of jump

To Decrease Difficulty

- Have players decrease the toss height.
- Slow the drill to a fast walk.
- Decrease the Success Goal.

To Increase Difficulty

- Have players increase the toss height.
- Have players increase their jogging speed.
- Increase the Success Goal.

3. Toss and Catch

[Corresponds to *Soccer*, Step 8, Drill 3]

Group Management and Safety Tips

- Position groups 5 yards apart.
- Have students self-pace the drill.

Equipment

- 1 ball per student pair

Instructions to Class

- "Face a partner at 5 yards and toss a ball back and forth. Receive each toss using the HEH principle (hands, eyes, and head aligned with the ball) with hands in the W position."
- "Toss the ball alternately to your partner's left and right."
- "Receive 40 tosses each."

Student Option

- "Vary the toss velocity."

Student Keys to Success

- Focus vision on the ball.
- Hands, eyes, and head aligned with the ball.
- Catch ball on fingertips with hands in W position.
- Cushion impact by withdrawing arms toward body.

Student Success Goal

- 35 or more tosses caught and held with hands in W position

To Decrease Difficulty

- Move partners closer.
- Require players to toss very softly.
- Reduce the Success Goal.

To Increase Difficulty

- Move partners farther apart.
- Require players to toss hard and with spin.
- Increase the Success Goal.

4. Volley and Catch

[Corresponds to *Soccer*, Step 8, Drill 4]

Group Management and Safety Tips

- Position groups several yards apart.
- Have students volley in the same direction.
- Have students self-pace the drill.

Equipment

- 1 ball per student pair

Instructions to Class

- "Face a partner at 10 yards and volley a ball back and forth. Catch each volley shot using the HEH principle with hands in the W position."
- "Catch the ball on your fingertips, not your palms."

- "Cushion the impact by withdrawing your hands and arms as the ball contacts your fingertips."
- "Receive 40 volley shots each."

Student Options

- "Use either the full or half volley, whichever comes easier."
- "Move closer together if you are having difficulty volleying."

Student Keys to Success

- Focus vision on ball.
- Hands, eyes, and head align with ball.

- Catch the ball on fingertips with hands in W position.
- Cushion ball impact.

Student Success Goal

- 32 or more volley shots received and held

To Decrease Difficulty

- Have students volley softly.
- Decrease the Success Goal.

To Increase Difficulty

- Move partners closer and instruct the server to volley with more velocity.
- Increase the Success Goal.

5. *Kneeling Save to Side*
[Corresponds to *Soccer*, Step 8, Drill 6]

Group Management and Safety Tips

- Position groups 10 yards apart.
- Have students self-pace the drill.

Equipment

- 1 ball per student pair

Instructions to Class

- "This drill lets you practice receiving a rolling ball to the side. Face a partner about 10 yards away."
- "Serve a rolling ball about 2 yards to your partner's left. Your partner moves laterally, drops to one knee, and receives the ball using proper technique. He or she rolls the ball back, a couple yards to your right. Receive the ball using correct technique and then return it 2 yards to your partner's right. Continue rolling the ball back and forth with your partner—left, right, right, left, left, right and so forth."
- "Each player receives 10 balls to the left and 10 to the right."

Student Options

- "Vary the serve velocity."
- "Vary the serve distance."

Student Keys to Success

- Move laterally to intercept the ball.
- Extend the lead foot toward the ball; kneel on the trailing leg.
- Leave only a few inches between the lead heel and the trailing knee.
- Let the ball roll up onto the wrists and forearms.
- Clutch the ball to your chest.

Student Success Goals

- 8 of 10 balls properly received to right side
- 8 of 10 balls properly received to left side

To Decrease Difficulty

- Reduce serve velocity.
- Decrease the Success Goal.

To Increase Difficulty

- Increase serve velocity.
- Increase the Success Goal.

6. Post to Post

[Corresponds to *Soccer*, Step 8, Drill 7]

Group Management and Safety Tip

- Mark an 8-yard wide goal for each group of three players.

Equipment

- 1 ball per group
- Cones, flags, or other markers for goalposts

Instructions to Class

- "Organize into groups of three. Two students in each group (A and B) act as servers while the remaining player is goalkeeper. Server A faces the right goalpost and B the left from 10 yards. The goalkeeper stands near the right goalpost and faces Server A."
- "Server A rolls the ball toward the goal center. The goalkeeper shuffles to his or her left, receives the ball using a kneeling save, and then tosses the ball to Server B before continuing across the goal. When the goalkeeper reaches the left goalpost, Server B rolls the ball toward the goal center. The keeper shuffles sideways, performs a kneeling save, tosses the ball to Server A, and continues to the right goalpost."
- "Goalkeepers do not cross their legs when shuffling across the goal mouth."
- "Continue until the goalkeeper receives 10 balls to the right and 10 to the left, then rotate positions and repeat. Everyone takes a turn as goalkeeper."

Student Option

- "Vary the serve velocity."

Student Keys to Success

- Move laterally across the goal.
- Extend the lead foot toward the ball and kneel on the trailing leg.
- Leave only a few inches between the lead heel and the trailing knee.
- Let the ball roll up onto wrists and forearms.
- Clutch the ball to your chest.

Student Success Goal

- 18 of 20 balls received without error

To Decrease Difficulty

- Decrease goal size.
- Decrease the speed of repetition.
- Decrease the Success Goal.

To Increase Difficulty

- Increase serve velocity.
- Increase the speed of repetition.
- Increase the Success Goal.

7. Four-Player Drill

[Corresponds to *Soccer*, Step 8, Drill 8]

Group Management and Safety Tips

- Organize students into groups of four. One or two groups can have an odd number of players depending upon class size.
- Position groups several yards apart.
- Do not leave balls lying unattended: A student could land on one after jumping to catch a high ball.
- Have students self-pace the drill.

Equipment

- 3 balls per group

Instructions to Class

- "Divide into groups of four. Three students in each group are servers and one is the goalkeeper. Servers encircle the goalkeeper about 15 yards away."
- "Each server, in turn, tosses a ball high into the center of the circle. The goalkeeper uses a one-leg takeoff to leap up and catch the ball at the highest point of the jump, then returns the ball to the server. Continue until the goalkeeper receives 30 high balls."

- "Remember to extend your arms and hands up over your head to catch the ball at the highest point of the jump."
- "Repeat until everyone has been goalkeeper once."

Student Option

- "Vary the toss height and trajectory."

Student Keys to Success

- Step toward the ball.
- Use a one-leg takeoff to jump up.
- Extend arms and hands above head.
- Keep head steady with vision on the ball.
- Catch the ball at highest point of the jump.

Student Success Goal

- 25 or more balls caught at highest point of jump

To Decrease Difficulty

- Require goalkeeper merely to extend arms and hands above the head to catch the ball (not jump).
- Decrease the Success Goal.

To Increase Difficulty

- Increase the speed of repetition.
- At circle center, set an extra student as an obstacle that the goalkeeper must jump over to catch the ball.

8. Diving to Save

[Corresponds to *Soccer*, Step 8, Drills 9 and 10]

Group Management and Safety Tips

- Have students practice diving on a soft surface: a padded mat indoors or a soft grass surface outdoors.
- Require students to wear long-sleeved shirts and (if available) light hip pads.
- Position students several yards apart so they can safely dive a couple yards to either side.

Equipment

- 2 balls per student

Instructions to Class

- "This exercise lets us practice diving to save a shot. Each of you get 2 soccer balls."
- "Kneel with a ball placed on each side within reach. Practice falling to your left, then right, to save the stationary ball. Land on your side, not your stomach. Pin the ball to the ground with one hand behind and one on top of it."
- "Repeat 10 times to each side, then position the balls 1 or 2 yards farther away. Repeat the drill but this time dive from a squat position. Dive 10 times to each side."

Student Option

- "You may have a classmate roll the ball slowly to your side and practice falling sideways from your knees to make the save."

Student Keys to Success

- Fall to side.
- Extend arms toward ball.
- Land on side as forearms and hips contact ground.
- Pin ball to ground with one hand on top and one behind.

Student Success Goals

- 18 or more correct dives from knees
- 16 or more correct dives from squat position

To Decrease Difficulty

- Decrease repetitions.
- Decrease the Success Goal.

To Increase Difficulty

- Increase speed of repetitions.
- Increase repetitions.
- Use rolling rather than stationary ball.
- Increase the Success Goal.

9. Standing Dive

[Corresponds to *Soccer*, Step 8, Drill 11]

Group Management and Safety Tips

- Practice on a soft surface: a padded mat indoors or a soft grass field or sawdust pit outdoors.
- Require students to wear long-sleeved shirts and (if available) light hip pads.
- Position student groups several yards apart so that they can safely dive 2 to 3 yards to either side.

Equipment

- 1 ball per student pair

Instructions to Class

- "Stand facing a partner 10 yards away. One partner is a goalkeeper, and the other a server. The goalkeeper assumes the ready position."
- "The server tosses a waist-high ball 2 to 3 yards to the side of the goalkeeper. The keeper dives sideways, catches the ball, and returns it to the server. After the goalkeeper regains the ready position, the server tosses the ball to the other side."
- "Dive on your side, not your stomach."
- "Hold the ball firmly in your hands so it does not bounce away when you hit the ground."
- "Dive 10 times to each side, then switch roles."

Student Options

- "Vary the serve velocity."
- "Vary the speed of repetition."

Student Keys to Success

- Assume the ready position.
- Step toward the ball, then push off with lead foot to vault sideways.
- Extend arms and hands toward the ball.
- Focus vision on the ball.
- Catch ball in hands, land on side.
- Pin ball to ground, then pull it to your chest.

Student Success Goals

- 7 of 10 balls caught and held when diving right
- 7 of 10 balls caught and held when diving left

To Decrease Difficulty

- Move partners closer.
- Have server throw very soft tosses.
- Reduce the Success Goal.

To Increase Difficulty

- Have server vary the service trajectory and add velocity.
- Increase the speed of repetition.
- Require longer dives to make the save.
- Increase the Success Goal.

10. Four Goal Game

[New Drill]

Group Management and Safety Tips

- Use markers to outline a 50-by-50-yard area for each game. Center a regulation-width goal on each sideline.
- Divide the class into equal teams of six to eight players each.

Equipment

- Cones, flags, or similar markers
- Regulation goals (or designate with cones)
- 1 ball per game
- Colored scrimmage vests to differentiate teams

Instructions to Class

- "Two teams will play per field. Each team defends two goals and can score in the other two. In each goal, teams position a goalkeeper who attempts to save all shots."
- "Kickoff from the center of the playing field. Teams score by shooting the ball through an opponent's goal. Regular soccer rules apply except that the offside rule is waived. The defending team gains possession through pass interception,

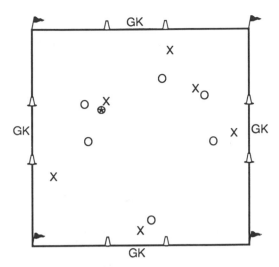

balls played out-of-bounds by the attacking team, or opposing team scores. The goalkeeper distributes the ball to a teammate after making a save."

- "Play for 20 minutes. Total the goals scored."

Student Option

- None

Student Keys to Success (Goalkeepers)

- Prepare to save all shots.
- Assume the ready position when the ball enters shooting range.
- Don't give up rebounds.
- Distribute the ball to a teammate to initiate the attack.

Goalkeeper Success Goal

- No goals allowed during a 20-minute game.

To Decrease Difficulty

- Decrease goal size.
- Reduce the Success Goal.

To Increase Difficulty

- Increase goal size.

11. Partner Throw

[Corresponds to *Soccer*, Step 8, Drill 12]

Group Management and Safety Tips

- Have goalkeepers distribute the ball in the same direction.
- Emphasize accuracy.

Equipment

- 1 ball per student pair

Instructions to Class

- "Choose a partner and practice the different methods of goalkeeper distribution by rolling or throwing the ball back and forth. Position 15 yards apart for rolling balls, 30 yards for the baseball throw, and 45 yards for the javelin throw."
- "A throw is considered accurate if the receiver must move no more than 3 steps to field it."
- "Execute 20 repetitions of each distribution method. Award yourself 1 point for each accurate throw."

Student Option

- "Position closer together if you physically cannot toss the ball the required distance."

Student Keys to Success

- Face the receiver.
- Step toward the target.
- Roll or throw the ball to the receiver's feet.

Student Success Goals

- 18 of 20 possible points rolling the ball
- 16 of 20 possible points using the baseball throw
- 14 of 20 possible points using the javelin throw

To Decrease Difficulty

- Move partners closer.
- Define an accurate throw as one within 5 steps of the receiver.
- Decrease the Success Goal.

To Increase Difficulty

- Increase distance between players.
- Define an accurate throw as one within 2 steps of the receiver.
- Increase the Success Goal.

12. *Throw to Hit the Fox*
[New Drill]

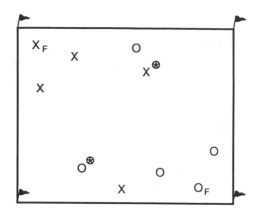

Group Management and Safety Tips

- Use markers to outline an area about 40 by 50 yards for each game.
- Divide class into equal teams of 5 to 8 players.
- Designate 1 player on each team as the *fox*.
- Establish a rule that all throws be aimed at the foxes' legs.

Equipment

- Cones, flags, or similar markers
- Colored scrimmage vests to differentiate teams
- Hats or other distinctive clothing to differentiate foxes from other players
- 2 balls per game

Instructions to Class

- "This drill emphasizes accurate distribution of the ball by throwing."
- "Two teams compete in a playing area. Each team has a ball to begin."
- "Teams score points by hitting the opposing fox with a thrown ball. Passing among teammates occurs by throwing and catching: Kicking is prohibited. Players may take only three steps while they have the ball before passing to a teammate or throwing at the fox. Teams protect their foxes by blocking or catching throws aimed at them. Change of possession occurs when a player intercepts a pass thrown by the other team, a player makes an errant throw and the ball touches the ground, or a player takes too many steps while in possession of the ball."
- "Keep both soccer balls in play at all times."
- "Players score 1 point for their team each time their throw hits the opposing fox. The ball must hit below the knees to count."
- "Play for 15 minutes. The team that scores the most points wins."

Student Option

- "Choose between the javelin and baseball throws when attempting to hit the fox."

Student Keys to Success

- Interpass to move the ball closer to the opposing fox.
- Use proper throwing technique.
- Aim throws at the feet.

Team Success Goal

- More points scored than opponents.

To Decrease Difficulty

- Use two extra balls.

To Increase Difficulty

- Use only one ball per game.

13. *Punting*

[Corresponds to *Soccer*, Step 8, Drills 13 and 14]

Group Management and Safety Tips

- Play on a regulation soccer field if possible.
- Organize students into pairs. Partners face off at 40 to 50 yards.
- Keep at least 5 yards between groups.
- Allow students to self-pace the drill.

Equipment

- 1 ball per student pair

Instructions to Class

- ''Face a partner at 40 yards and punt a ball back and forth.''
- ''You receive 1 point for each punt that hits the ground within 5 yards of your partner.''
- ''Punt 30 times each.''

Student Option

- None

Student Keys to Success

- Square shoulders with target.
- Extend arms and hold the ball at about waist level.
- Keep head steady with vision on the ball.
- Kick up through the ball's center with the instep of the foot.
- Follow through completely.

Student Success Goal

- 25 or more points scored

To Decrease Difficulty

- Move partners closer.
- Reduce the Success Goal.

To Increase Difficulty

- Move partners farther apart.
- Increase the Success Goal.

Step 9 Small Group Strategies in Attack

A primary attack objective in soccer is to position more attackers than defenders near the ball. Once this numerical superiority is established, attackers must work in combination to advance the ball past the defenders. Two small group strategies, the *give and go pass* and *support*, commonly help achieve that aim.

The foundation for attacking group tactics is the two-versus-one situation—two attackers versus one defender. The give and go (or wall) pass provides the most effective means of beating the defender in a two-versus-one situation. To successfully execute the give and go pass the two attackers each perform different duties, yet work in unison.

Adding a third attacker to the situation (three-versus-one) provides *support* in the attack. To support the player with the ball, teammates move near the ball to become passing options. Key factors of offensive support are the number of support players, the angle of support, and the distance of support.

Give and Go Pass Rating: Passer

BEGINNING LEVEL	ADVANCED LEVEL
Preparation	
• Has poor control of ball	• Quickly controls ball and faces defender
• Misses give and go pass opportunities	• Immediately recognizes chance for give and go pass
Execution	
• Delays dribbling at defender	• Immediately dribbles at defender
• Dribbles diagonally away from defender	• Takes shortest route to goal
• Keeps ball past chance for give and go pass or passes before defender commits to tackle	• Passes to support player (wall) at moment when defender closes to tackle
• Passes with inside of foot	• Passes with outside of foot
• Passes behind support player	• Passes to lead foot of support player
Follow-Through	
• Runs wide of defender out of position to receive return pass	• Sprints forward into space behind defender

Give and Go Pass Rating: Receiver

BEGINNING LEVEL	ADVANCED LEVEL
Preparation • Improper support position rules out give and go pass • Positions too far away from player with ball, or behind or in front of defender	• Moves toward player with ball • Positions 3 to 4 yards to side of defender
Execution • Foot weakly positioned when redirecting ball into space behind defender • Stops ball	• Uses lead foot as ''wall'' to redirect pass into space behind defender • Plays ball first time (one touch) into space behind defender
Follow-Through • Remains stationary after passing ball	• Sprints forward after redirecting ball to teammate in space behind defender

Support Rating

BEGINNING LEVEL	ADVANCED LEVEL
Preparation • Positions at too great a distance from teammate with ball • Positions directly behind opponent • Forms a narrow angle of support with another supporting teammate (less than 90 degrees)	• Positions near teammate with ball • Positions with open passing lane to ball • Forms a wide angle of support with another supporting teammate (90 degrees or more)
Execution • Remains positioned despite movements of defender and ball • Remains positioned after ball is passed to another player	• Maintains wide angle of support • Assumes new support position when ball is passed to a nearby teammate
Follow-Through • Head down with vision on ball • Remains positioned despite changing location of ball	• Keeps head up with vision on surrounding players • Assumes new support position in response to changing position of ball.

Error Detection and Correction for Small Group Attacking Strategies

Because group attacking strategies provide the foundation for higher level team tactics you should spend as much time as possible refining these concepts. Give and go pass errors may occur for a variety of reasons.

- Failure of the dribbler to commit the defender
- Failure to pass at the correct moment
- Pass inaccuracies

- Improper position of the support player
- Failure of the dribbler to sprint forward after passing to the support player

Errors in support usually result from incorrect positioning of support players in relation to the ball and defender(s). As you observe students focus your attention and comments on these common errors in performance.

ERROR

CORRECTION

1. The dribbler fails to commit the defender.

1. The dribbler must initiate play. Tell him or her to immediately take on the defender upon seeing a give and go pass opportunity, and then pass the ball the instant the defender closes to tackle.

2. The dribbler passes behind the support player.

2. The support player cannot one-touch the ball into the space behind the defender if the ball is passed behind him or her. Therefore the ball must be passed to the support player's lead foot.

3. The support player positions incorrectly.

3. Have the support player position for an open passing lane to the ball. Tell the support player to position to the side of, not behind, the defender.

4. Support players fail to reposition when the ball changes location.

4. Teach students that the proper angle of support depends upon the ball's location in relation to defenders. As the ball changes location so does the correct angle and distance of support. Demonstrate how the support players constantly reposition as the ball moves. Try Drill 2.

5. Two or more attackers are each covered by a single defender.

5. This occurs when support players position either too close to the dribbler or behind defenders. Explain that distance and angle of support are critical factors that must constantly be reevaluated and adjusted to specific situations.

Small Group Attacking Drills

1. *Playing the Wall*
[Corresponds to *Soccer*, Step 9, Drill 1]

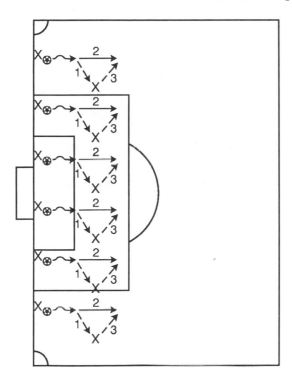

Group Management and Safety Tips

- Have all students jog in the same direction.
- Keep 10 yards between groups.
- Have students perform the drill at half speed. Emphasize proper execution: The drill is not a race.

Equipment

- 1 ball per student pair

Instructions to Class

- "Pair up and position along the endline with a ball. Practice the give and go pass with your partner against an imaginary defender while jogging the length of the field."
- "The dribbler receives 1 point for each successful pass to the lead foot of the support player (the wall). The support player receives 1 point for each one-touch pass directed into the space behind the imaginary defender."
- "Remember to target the first pass to the support player's lead foot; and the second into the space behind the imaginary defender."
- "Execute 30 wall passes, then switch roles with your partner and perform 30 more."
- "Perform the drill first at half speed, then speed up as you become more proficient."

Student Option

- "Practice to both sides, with the support player first to the dribbler's right, then left."

Student Keys to Success

Dribbler

- Dribble toward the imaginary defender.
- Pass to the support player's lead foot.
- Sprint forward after passing.

Support Player

- Position beside imaginary defender.
- Use open stance.
- Firmly position your lead foot and one-touch the ball into the space behind the defender.
- Move forward to support the ball.

Student Success Goals

- 25 or more points when dribbling
- 25 or more points when supporting

To Decrease Difficulty

- Practice with a stationary partner.
- Decrease the Success Goal.

To Increase Difficulty

- Increase execution speed.
- Add a passive defender.
- Increase the Success Goal.

2. Shadow Drill (3 vs. 0)
[Corresponds to *Soccer*, Step 9, Drill 2]

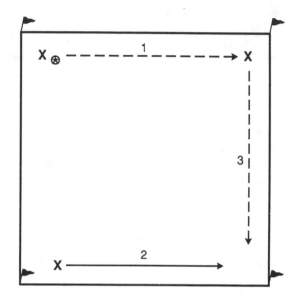

Group Management and Safety Tips

- Use markers to outline a 10-by-10 yard grid for each group.
- Keep at least 5 yards between grids.
- Caution students to stay out of other grids when chasing a stray ball.

Equipment

- 1 ball per group of 3 players
- Cones, flags, or similar markers to outline the grids

Instructions to Class

- "Organize into groups of three with one ball per group. Each group plays in a 10-by-10-yard grid."
- "Position in three adjacent corners of the grid. The player with the ball should have a teammate on either side."
- "The player with the ball passes to either teammate. The teammate not receiving the ball immediately runs to the corner that is unoccupied and adjacent to the ball. The player who received the ball in turn passes it to this player and the teammate who began the cycle moves to an adjacent corner of the grid."
- "Remember that the player with the ball should always have a supporting teammate in each adjacent corner. As the ball moves so does the support player."
- "Continue until each player has made 20 passes and 20 supporting runs."

Student Options

- "Increase the speed as you become more proficient."
- "The player with the ball may pass to either support player."

Student Keys to Success

- Quickly reposition as the ball changes position.
- Recognize the wide angle of support.
- Pass the ball along the ground.
- Control and pass with the fewest possible touches.

Student Success Goal

- 20 out of 20 correct support runs responding to the ball's changing position

To Decrease Difficulty

- Have students use a fast walk.
- Decrease the Success Goal.

To Increase Difficulty

- Increase execution speed.
- Limit the number of touches permitted to control and pass.
- Increase the grid size to increase physical demands.

3. Two Versus One in the Grid

[Corresponds to *Soccer*, Step 9, Drill 3]

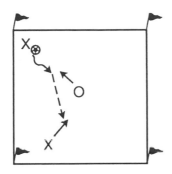

Group Management and Safety Tips

- Use markers to outline a 10-by-10-yard grid for each group.
- Position grids at least 5 yards apart.
- Caution players to stay out of other grids when chasing stray balls.
- Prohibit slide tackles.

Equipment

- 1 ball per group of 3 players
- Cones, flags, or similar markers to outline areas

Instructions to Class

- "This drill provides practice of the give and go pass. Organize into groups of three. Each group positions in a grid."
- "Two attackers compete against one defender in each grid. The attackers try to maintain ball possession from the defender by using dribbling, shielding, and passing skills."
- "The attackers receive 2 points for each successful give and go pass within the grid, and 1 point for five consecutive passes without loss of possession. The defender receives 1 point for intercepting a pass, tackling the ball, or forcing the attackers to play the ball out of the grid. The

defender immediately returns the ball to the attackers after stealing it so the game can continue without interruption. The defender cannot slide tackle the ball."
- "Play for 10 minutes, then select a new defender for the next drill repetition. Total the points scored for attackers and the defender. I will signal the start and end of the drill."

Student Options

- "Choose a new defender for each 10-minute period."
- "The defender chooses between block and poke tackles to gain possession."

Student Keys to Success (for Attackers)

- Work together to beat the defender.
- When supporting, position with an open passing lane to the dribbler.
- When dribbling, commit the defender, pass to the support player, then sprint behind the defender to receive a return pass.

Team Success Goal

- More points scored than defender.

To Decrease Difficulty

- Increase grid size.
- Award attackers 1 point for three consecutive passes without loss of possession.

To Increase Difficulty

- Decrease grid size.
- Award attackers 1 point for seven consecutive passes without loss of possession.
- Limit attackers to two touches to control and pass.

4. Keep-Away Game (3 vs. 1)
[Corresponds to *Soccer*, Step 9, Drill 4]

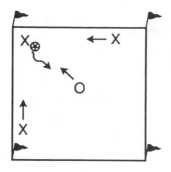

Group Management and Safety Tips

- Use markers to outline a 10-by-10-yard grid for each group of four.
- Position grids at least 5 yards apart.
- Caution students to stay out of other grids when chasing a stray ball.
- Prohibit slide tackles.

Equipment

- 1 ball per group of 4 players
- Cones, flags, or similar markers to outline grid areas

Instructions to Class

- "Organize into groups of four. Designate one group member as defender and the remaining three as attackers. Each group positions in a grid."
- "The three attackers try to keep the ball away from the defender within the grid boundaries. The attacking team receives 1 point for 10 consecutive passes in the grid without loss of possession. The at-tackers must receive and pass in four or fewer touches. A defender who steals the ball immediately returns it to the attackers so the drill continues uninterrupted. The defender cannot slide tackle the ball."
- "Play for 5 minutes after which we will switch defenders and repeat the drill. Total the attackers' points. I will signal the start and end of the drill."

Student Options

- "Use any appropriate passing skill."
- "The defender chooses between block and poke tackles."

Student Keys to Success

- Use accurate passing and ball control.
- When supporting, use proper positioning in relation to the ball and defender.
- Wisely decide when and where to pass the ball and where to move after passing it.

Team Success Goal

- 5 or more points scored in a 5-minute game

To Decrease Difficulty

- Increase grid size.
- Allow the attackers unlimited touches.
- Reduce the Success Goal.

To Increase Difficulty

- Decrease grid size.
- Limit the attackers to two touches.
- Increase the Success Goal.

5. Two Versus One to the Line
[Corresponds to *Soccer*, Step 9, Drill 5]

Group Management and Safety Tips

- Use markers to outline a lane 15 yards wide for each group.
- Caution students to avoid other groups when chasing a stray ball.

Equipment

- 1 ball per group of 3 players
- Cones or flags to designate a lane for each group

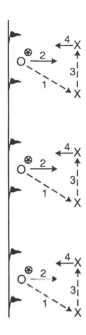

Instructions to Class

- "Organize into groups of three. Designate two players as attackers and one as defender. The attackers position about 25 yards from a touchline or endline of the field while the defender stands on the line with the ball."
- "The defender kicks the ball to the attackers and then immediately moves off of the line to intercept the attackers. Meanwhile the attackers control the ball and attempt to beat the defender to the line by using a give and go pass. The attackers must remain in the 15-yard-wide lane to beat the defender."
- "The attackers receive 1 point for beating the defender to the line within the 15-yard-wide zone. Repeat the drill 10 times, then choose a new defender."

Student Option

- "The defender may serve the ball along the ground or chip it through the air."

Student Keys to Success (for Attackers)

- When dribbling, take on the defender.
- When supporting, position to the defender's side.
- When dribbling, commit the defender before passing to a support player.
- After passing, sprint forward into the space behind the defender.
- When receiving, one-touch the ball into the open space behind the defender.

Team Success Goal

- 7 or more points scored

To Decrease Difficulty

- Increase zone width.
- Decrease the Success Goal.

To Increase Difficulty

- Decrease zone width.
- Increase the Success Goal.

6. *Two Versus One Plus One*

[Corresponds to *Soccer*, Step 9, Drill 6]

Group Management and Safety Tips

- Use markers to outline a 20-by-30-yard grid for each game. Position 4-yard-wide goals on each grid endline.
- Keep at least 5 yards between grids.

Equipment

- 1 ball per group of 4 players
- Cones, flags, or similar markers

Instructions to Class

- "Organize into teams of two. Two teams position in each grid. Each team defends a goal and scores by kicking the ball through the opponent's goal. To begin, I will award one team ball possession."
- "The team with the ball attacks with two players while the opposing team defends with one player and uses the other as goalkeeper. If the defending team gains possession—either by winning a tackle or making a save—then the goalkeeper immediately joins his or her teammate to attack the opposing goal. Meanwhile, one of the former attackers immediately sprints back to become goalkeeper while the other teammate becomes defender."

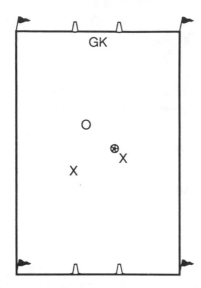

- "The game continues nonstop except for the brief delay of retrieving a ball that scored. Remember to always attack with two players and always defend with one defender and a goalkeeper."
- "A team receives 1 point for each give and go pass that beats an opponent, and 1 additional point for each goal scored. Play

for 15 minutes. I will signal the start and end of the drill."

Student Option

- "The goalkeeper can choose from all goalkeeping techniques to save shots."

Student Keys to Success

- Transition quickly from defense to attack after gaining ball possession.
- Player with ball immediately takes on defender.
- Support player positions for a give and go pass.
- Beat the defender with a give and go pass.
- Finish the attack with a goal.

Team Success Goal

- More points scored than opponents.

To Decrease Difficulty

- Increase goal size.

To Increase Difficulty

- Decrease goal size.
- Decrease field size.

7. *Three Versus One to Goal*
[Corresponds to *Soccer*, Step 9, Drill 7]

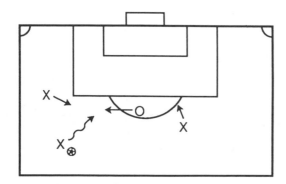

Group Management and Safety Tips

- Have each group play into a regulation goal. If actual goals are not available, designate goals with cones or flags.
- Prohibit slide tackling by the defender.

Equipment

- A regulation-size goal for each group
- 4 to 5 soccer balls per group

Instructions to Class

- "Organize into groups of four. Designate three players as attackers and one as defender. Attackers position 30 yards from goal with one ball. The defender positions to protect the goal. The attackers try to kick the ball through the goal to score."
- "The attackers use combination interpassing coupled with proper support movement to create scoring opportunities. The attackers receive 1 point for each goal scored and the defender receives 2 points for gaining possession. Defenders cannot

slide tackle the ball. After each score, or after the defender gains possession, the attackers restart the drill from their original spot 30 yards from goal.''

- ''Attackers must receive, pass, and shoot in three touches.''
- ''Play for 10 minutes. Total the points scored for attackers and the defender. I will signal the beginning and end of the drill.''

Student Option

- ''Add a goalkeeper if you wish.''

Student Keys to Success (for Attackers)

- When supporting, position properly.
- Use precise passing and ball control.

- Use the give and go pass to beat the defender.
- Finish each attack with a shot on goal.

Team Success Goal

- More points scored than defender.

To Decrease Difficulty

- Allow the attackers unlimited touches.
- Enlarge the goal.

To Increase Difficulty

- Limit the attackers to two touches.
- Decrease goal size.
- Add a goalkeeper.

8. *Splitting the Defense*
[New Drill]

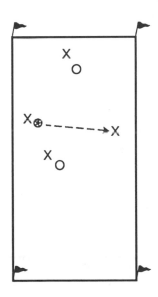

Group Management and Safety Tips

- Use markers to outline a 12-by-24-yard grid for each group.
- Divide students into groups of six.
- Designate four attackers and two defenders for each group.
- Prohibit slide tackles.

Equipment

- Cones, flags, or similar markers

- Colored scrimmage vests to differentiate attackers from defenders
- 1 ball per group

Instructions to Class

- ''Each group positions in a 12-by-24-yard grid. The four attackers try to maintain ball possession from the defenders. Attackers score 1 point for completing 10 consecutive passes and 2 points for completing a pass between two defenders.''
- ''Attackers must begin the count again if the defenders win ball possession or the ball is played out of the area. Defenders score 1 point for gaining possession, after which they return the ball to the attackers and the drill continues.''
- ''Do not use slide tackles.''
- ''Play for 15 minutes. Total the points for both attackers and defenders.''

Student Option

- None

Student Keys to Success (for Attackers)

- Spread out to utilize the width and depth of the playing area.

- Position at wide angles of support.
- Look to split the defenders with a pass whenever possible.

Team Success Goal

- More points scored than opponents.

To Decrease Difficulty

- Increase grid size.

To Increase Difficulty

- Reduce grid size.
- Add another defender.

9. Hot Potato
[New Drill]

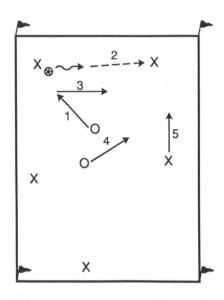

Group Management and Safety Tips

- Use markers to outline a 15-by-20-yard grid for each group.
- Divide students into groups of seven. Designate five attackers and two defenders in each group.
- Position grids at least 5 yards apart.

Equipment

- Cones, flags, or similar markers to designate grids
- Colored scrimmage vests to differentiate attackers from defenders
- 1 ball per group

Instructions to Class

- ''Attackers position around the area's perimeter and the two defenders position in the area's center.''

- ''The attackers try to maintain ball possession from the defenders by using only one- and two-touch passing. (The game is called *hot potato* because the ball is continually moving among players.) Attackers score 2 points for 12 consecutive passes; defenders score 1 point for each interception. A defender who steals the ball immediately returns it to the attacking team and the game continues.''
- ''The attackers are penalized 1 point if they kick the ball out of the area.''
- ''Play for 10 minutes. Total the points scored.''

Student Options

- None

Student Keys to Success (for Attackers)

- Provide support for the player with the ball.
- Position at wide angles of support.
- Use the entire playing area to spread defenders apart.
- Use proper player movement off the ball to create open passing lanes.

Team Success Goal

- More points scored than opponents.

To Decrease Difficulty

- Increase area size.
- Allow the attackers unlimited touches.

To Increase Difficulty

- Reduce area size.
- Add an extra defender.

Step 10 Small Group Strategies in Defense

Just as attackers work together to score, defenders must also collectively organize to prevent goals. To create this strong team defense, students must learn the strategies of defensive cover and balance. Defensive cover and balance require teamwork between two or more defending players.

Defensive cover is the defensive counterpart to offensive support in attack in that the defender nearest the ball (the first defender) should be supported, or covered, by a teammate. The supporting teammate (the second defender) must protect the space behind the first defender. The second defender also posi-tions to challenge for the ball should the first defender be beaten on the dribble. Thus the second defender functions like the free safety in American football, who is free to cover space and help teammates if needed.

Defensive balance is an extension of de-fensive cover. Balance is provided by one or more players (third defenders) who cover the space diagonally behind the second defender. Defensive balance protects the vulnerable space between the last line of defense and the goalkeeper. Teach your students the respon-sibilities of first, second, and third defenders, which are used in all systems of play.

First Defender Rating	
BEGINNING LEVEL	**ADVANCED LEVEL**
Preparation	
• Feet in square defensive stance	• Feet in staggered stance, shoulder-width apart
• Uncertain balance, body control, and movement	• Maintains balance and body control and moves quickly in any direction
• Applies little pressure to opponent with ball	• Positions to tackle ball that strays from dribbler's range of control
• Positions to side of dribbler's shortest route to goal	• Positions goalside of dribbler to block direct route to goal
Execution	
• Follows dribbler's movement without directing it away from goal	• Forces dribbler diagonally away from goal or into space covered by teammate
• Attempts to tackle ball before team-mate can cover	• Contains dribbler's forward progress
• Overcommits and is beaten on dribble	• Forces the dribbler to pass square across field or backward
• Allows dribbler to pass forward	• Prevents a penetrating pass or run
Follow-Through	
• Fails to recover goalside of dribbler	• Tackles ball and initiates attack

Second Defender Rating

BEGINNING LEVEL	ADVANCED LEVEL
Preparation	
• Positions far from first defender, leaving space behind open	• Positions 2 to 4 yards from first defender depending upon field area
• Directly behind first defender	• Diagonally behind and to side of first defender
• Disregards opponent in vicinity of ball	• Covers space behind first defender and marks opponent in vicinity of ball
• Allows ball or opponent being marked to stray from vision	• Always keeps ball and opponent being marked in vision
Execution	
• Remains stationary behind first defender when he or she is beaten	• Advances to challenge opponent who has beaten first defender
• Allows penetrating pass through space behind first defender	• Intercepts pass into space behind first defender
Follow-Through	
• Retains second-defender position when first defender is beaten	• Becomes first defender if original first defender is beaten
• Remains positioned as ball changes position	• Assumes new support position when ball is passed to different opponent

Third Defender Rating

BEGINNING LEVEL	ADVANCED LEVEL
Preparation	
• Positions close to second defender, leaving open space diagonally behind	• Covers space diagonally behind second defender
• Positions out of line of balance	• Positions along line of balance (line from ball position to far goalpost)
• Lets ball and nearby opponents stray from vision	• Always keeps ball and nearby opponents in vision
Execution	
• Allows penetrating pass into space behind second defender	• Prevents pass through space diagonally behind second defender; forces opponent to play ball square across field in front of defense
• Allows pass over head to attacker running to goal	• Prevents long diagonal pass to flank player running behind defense
Follow-Through	
• Retains position despite changing position of ball and teammates	• Constantly readjusts line of balance with changing position of ball and teammates

Error Detection and Correction for Small Group Strategies in Defense

Proper defensive cover and balance require coordinated movement of the first, second, and third defenders. Errors generally occur due to failure of the first defender to contain the dribbler, incorrect position of the second defender, incorrect position of the third defender, or a combination of these. As you observe students, focus especially on their positioning in relation to the ball and teammates. Provide corrective feedback emphasizing correct decision making.

ERROR ⊘   **CORRECTION**

First Defender

1. The first defender attempts to tackle the ball before the second defender can cover.

2. The first defender fails to tightly mark the dribbler.

1. Tell the first defender not to challenge for possession unless absolutely sure of winning the tackle or being supported from behind by the second defender.

2. Emphasize that correct marking distance is critical. Tell the first defender to mark more tightly as the ball moves closer to goal. The marking distance should be about 1 to 1-1/2 yards. At that distance the first defender can apply pressure while preventing the opponent from pushing the ball forward into open space and sprinting to it.

Second Defender

1. The second defender positions directly behind the first defender.

1. Emphasize that the second defender has two primary responsibilities: to protect the space behind and beside the first defender, and to mark an opponent near the ball. To accomplish both of those tasks the second defender should position diagonally behind the first defender. From that position the second defender can watch both the ball and the opponent being marked at the same time.

ERROR ⦸

CORRECTION

2. The second defender positions too close or too far from the first defender.

2. Determining correct cover distance is very important. Tell the second defender to position close enough to step forward and challenge an opponent who beats the first defender, yet not so close that an opponent can beat both defenders by pushing the ball past them and sprinting to it. Thus the second defender must consider the first defender's ability as well as the attacker's ability when determining proper cover distance.

Third Defender

1. The third defender leaves open the space behind the second defender.

1. Have the third defender position along a line of balance that extends from the ball to the far goalpost. Make sure the student knows that the line of balance changes as the ball moves.

2. The third defender positions too close to the second defender.

2. The third defender must prevent long crossfield passes behind the defense and intercept any ball passed into the space directly behind the second defender. The third defender must therefore position at the proper distance from the second defender to fulfill both responsibilities.

Defensive Cover and Balance Drills

1. Cover the Goal
[Corresponds to *Soccer*, Step 10, Drill 1]

Group Management and Safety Tips
• Use markers to outline a 10-by-15-yard grid for each student group. Position a goal 4 yards wide on one end of each grid, and a zone 3 yards wide across the center of the grid.

• Leave at least 5 yards between grids.

Equipment
• 1 ball per group of 3 students
• Cones, flags, or similar markers to designate grids and goals

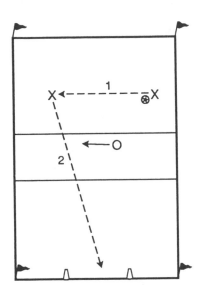

Instructions to Class

- "Organize into groups of three and position in a grid. Designate two players as attackers and one as defender."
- "One attacker positions in each corner of the grid opposite the goal. The defender positions in the center of the grid and faces the attackers. The attackers try to create an open passing lane to the goal by quickly passing the ball back and forth to draw the defender out of position. The defender tries to prevent the attackers from passing the ball through the goal by quickly responding to the changing position of the ball."

- "The defender must stay within a 3-yard zone marked across the grid's center. He or she cannot tackle the ball. The attackers cannot move toward the goal but must stay in their respective corners of the grid."
- "The attackers receive 1 point if they kick the ball past the defender and through the goal. The defender receives 1 point for each forward pass that he or she intercepts. Total the points scored during 5 minutes of play."
- "I will signal the start and end of each 5-minute period."

Student Option

- None

Student Keys to Success (for Defender)

- Use balance and body control.
- Use quick lateral movement.
- Maintain position between ball and goal.

Student Success Goal (for Defender)

- More points scored than attackers.

To Decrease Difficulty (for Defender)

- Decrease grid width.
- Decrease goal width.

To Increase Difficulty (for Defender)

- Increase grid width.
- Increase goal width.
- Allow the attackers to move out of their corners to pass.

2. Two Versus Two

[Corresponds to *Soccer*, Step 10, Drill 2]

Group Management and Safety Tips

- Use markers to outline a 10-by-15-yard grid for each group. Position a goal 4 yards wide on each endline of the grid.
- Keep at least 5 yards between grids.

Equipment

- 1 ball per group of 4 players
- Cones, flags, or similar markers to designate grids and goals

Instructions to Class

- "This drill emphasizes correct defensive cover. Organize into teams of two. Two teams compete in each 15-by-20-yard grid. I will award one team ball possession to begin the drill."
- "Teams score by kicking the ball through the opponent's goal. When your team is on defense, the first defender must apply pressure on the dribbler. The second

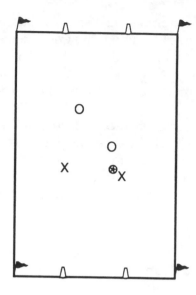

defender provides cover to prevent a shot past the first defender through the goal. The second defender must also mark the opponent who does not have the ball.''
- ''Play until one team scores 10 goals.''

Student Option

- ''A ball that goes out of bounds can be returned to play by a throw-in or kick-in.''

Student Keys to Success

- The first defender positions goalside of the dribbler.
- The second defender protects the space behind the first defender and blocks the passing lane to goal.
- Defending players work in tandem to quickly shift roles depending upon which opponent has the ball.

Team Success Goal

- Fewer goals allowed than opponents.

To Decrease Difficulty (for Defenders)

- Make field smaller.
- Make goals smaller.

To Increase Difficulty (for Defenders)

- Make field larger.
- Make goals larger.

3. *Three Versus Two*
[Corresponds to *Soccer*, Step 10, Drill 3]

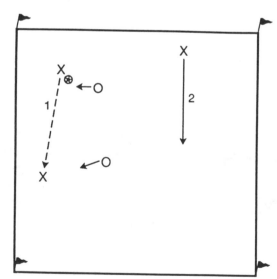

Group Management and Safety Tips

- Use markers to outline a 15-by-15-yard grid for each group.
- Keep at least 5 yards between grids.

Equipment

- 1 ball per group of 5 students
- Cones, flags, or similar markers to outline grid areas
- Colored scrimmage vests to differentiate teams

Instructions to Class

- ''Organize into groups of five. Designate three players as attackers and two as defenders. Position in a 15-by-15-yard grid.''
- ''The attackers pass the ball among themselves and try to keep away from the defenders within the grid. The attackers receive 1 point for 10 passes completed in succession, or 2 points for a pass that splits (goes between) the defenders. The defenders receive 1 point for gaining possession or forcing the attackers to play the ball out of the grid. Defenders must not

use slide tackles. Defenders immediately return stolen balls to attackers and the game continues.''
- ''Because defenders are outnumbered they must work together to prevent attackers from scoring points. The first defender applies pressure on the dribbler while the second defender positions to prevent a pass that splits the defense.''
- ''Play for 10 minutes. I will signal the start and end of the drill.''

Student Option

- ''Defenders may use block or poke tackles to gain ball possession.''

Student Keys to Success

Defenders

- First defender: Pressure the dribbler.
- Limit the passing options of dribbler.

- Second defender: Cover the space behind the first defender and prevent a pass that splits the defense.

Attackers

- Use precise passing and ball control.
- Draw defenders out of position.

Team Success Goal

- More points scored than opponents.

To Decrease Difficulty (for Defenders)

- Reduce playing-area size.
- Limit attackers to two touches to receive and pass.

To Increase Difficulty (for Defenders)

- Increase playing-area size.

4. *Three Versus Two Plus One*

[Corresponds to *Soccer*, Step 10, Drill 4]

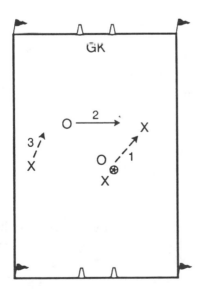

Group Management and Safety Tips

- Use markers to outline a 20-by-30-yard grid for each group. Position a goal 4 yards wide on each endline of the grid.
- Keep at least 5 yards between grids.

- Caution defenders to stay on their feet. Because of potential injury, prohibit slide tackles.

Equipment

- 1 ball per game
- Cones, flags, or similar markers
- Colored scrimmage vests to differentiate teams

Instructions to Class

- ''Organize into teams of three. Match up against another team in a 20-by-30-yard grid. I will award one team ball possession to begin the drill.''
- ''The team with the ball attacks with all three players while the opposing team defends with two field players and a goalkeeper. After a goal is scored or when the defending team gains possession, teams switch roles. The former defending team attacks with three players as the goalkeeper joins the field players. One

member of the former attacking team guards the goal and the other two field players defend. Teams receive 1 point for each goal scored.''

- ''When a defender steals the ball, he or she must pass it to the goalkeeper before the goalkeeper can join the attack.''
- ''Remember your defense responsibilities. The first defender pressures the dribbler while the second defender covers the space behind the first defender. Defenders constantly adjust to the changing ball position.''
- ''Play for 15 minutes. I will signal the start and end of the game.''

Student Option

- ''Use a throw-in or kick-in to return a ball that leaves the playing area.''

Student Keys to Success

Defenders

- First defender: Pressure the dribbler.

- Second defender: Cover the space behind the first defender.
- Use verbal communication.

Attackers

- Position at wide angles of support.
- Use precise passing and ball control.
- Use give and go pass when appropriate.

Team Success Goal

- Fewer goals allowed than opponents.

To Decrease Difficulty (for Defending Team)

- Decrease field size.
- Decrease goal size.
- Limit touches attackers can use to pass and receive.

To Increase Difficulty (for Defending Team)

- Increase field size.
- Increase goal size.

5. *Prevent the Killer Pass*
[Corresponds to *Soccer*, Step 10, Drill 6]

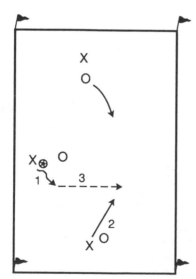

Group Management and Safety Tips

- Use markers to outline a 20-by-30-yard grid for each group.
- Keep at least 5 yards between grids.
- Prohibit slide tackles.

Equipment

- 1 ball per game
- Cones, flags, or similar markers to outline grids
- Colored scrimmage vests to differentiate teams

Instructions to Class

- ''Organize into teams of three. Match up against another team to play three versus three in a 20-by-30-yard grid. I will award one team ball possession to start the game.''
- ''The team with the ball tries to maintain possession from opponents in the grid boundaries. If defenders steal the ball or attackers pass the ball out of the playing area, teams immediately switch roles.''
- ''A team receives 1 point for eight consecutive passes without loss of possession and 2 points if its players make a 'killer

pass,' a pass that splits, or goes between, two defenders.''

- ''Defenders must work together to prevent opponents from scoring. The first defender pressures the opponent with the ball, the second positions to cover the space behind the first, and the third positions diagonally behind the second to provide balance.''
- ''Play for 15 minutes. Total the points scored. I will signal the start and end of the game.''

Student Option

- ''Use a throw-in or kick-in to return a ball that goes out of the playing area.''

Student Keys to Success (for Defenders)

- Limit passing options for the dribbler.
- Provide cover and balance to prevent killer passes.

Team Success Goal

- Fewer points allowed than opponents.

To Decrease Difficulty (for Defenders)

- Decrease playing-area size.
- Limit touches allowed attackers.

To Increase Difficulty (for Defenders)

- Increase playing-area size.

6. *Defending in an Outnumbered Situation*

[Corresponds to *Soccer*, Step 10, Drill 7]

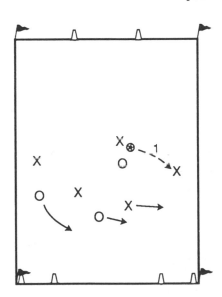

Group Management and Safety Tips

- Use markers to outline a 30-by-40-yard area for each group. Center a goal 6 yards wide on one endline. Position a goal 3 yards wide at each end of the opposite endline.

Equipment

- 1 ball per game
- Cones, flags, or similar markers
- Colored scrimmage vests to differentiate teams

Instructions to Class

- ''Organize into groups of eight. Divide into a team of five players and a team of three players. The five-player team defends the large goal and can score in either small goal. The three-player team defends the two small goals and can score in the large goal. Teams score by passing the ball through the correct goal below waist height.''
- ''The outnumbered team receives 2 points for each goal scored. The five-player team receives 1 point for each goal scored.''
- ''Do not use goalkeepers.''
- ''Total the points for each team.''
- ''Play for about 10 minutes. I will begin and end each drill.''

Student Option

- None

Student Keys to Success (for Outnumbered Team)

- Quickly assume first, second, and third defender roles.

- The first defender pressures the opponent with the ball.
- The second defender provides cover for the first defender.
- The third defender provides balance in defense.

Student Success Goal (Outnumbered Team)

- More points scored than opponents.

To Decrease Difficulty (Outnumbered Team)

- Decrease playing-area size.
- Impose a two-touch limit for the five-player team.

To Increase Difficulty (Outnumbered Team)

- Increase playing-area size.
- Increase size of goals defended by the outnumbered team.

Step 11 Attacking as a Team

A team will not consistently score unless players combine their efforts. To do so players must have a common set of criteria on which to base their decisions and subsequent behaviors. These criteria, commonly called the principles of attack, conceptualize the goals and objectives of attacking soccer and are universal to all systems of play. Teach your students the principles of attack, which they must use as a basis for decision making when their team has ball possession.

First and foremost, attacking strategies must create space and time, both on an individual and team basis. Your students already know the important relationship between space and time on the soccer field: The time available for decision making and skill execution is directly proportional to the space available. Furthermore, the more time an individual has to make decisions and execute skills, the greater the likelihood of success. Therefore the attacking team must create as much space as possible to maximize its scoring opportunities.

Your students learned the principles of team attack in *Soccer: Steps to Success*. Briefly review these principles: player movement, combination play, improvisation, total team support, and finishing the attack.

Error Detection and Correction for Attacking as a Team

Players must combine precise skill execution with correct decision making to create the teamwork necessary for scoring. This is not easy. Even experienced players sometimes become confused and make mistakes on split-second decisions.

Instruct all players to base their decisions on the same criteria. You can improve your students' decision-making abilities by providing them with a clear understanding of the principles underlying attacking soccer. As you observe students in game situations, focus on the decisions they make in response to changing situations. Refer to the principles of attack discussed in *Soccer: Steps to Success* when providing corrective feedback.

ERROR

CORRECTION

1. Students move around very little and are therefore easily marked by opponents.

1. Attackers must work hard to create space for themselves and teammates. Teach the player with ball to use checking movements to create sufficient space to turn on the defender. Encourage support players to use checking runs and diagonal runs to create sufficient space to receive a pass. Diagonal runs can also draw defenders out of position to clear space for teammates.

ERROR

CORRECTION

2. The attackers fail to utilize the field's flank areas.

2. The attackers must create open spaces in the opponent's defense. Have attackers position to stretch the opposing team vertically down the field and horizontally across the field (providing width and depth).

3. The attackers consistently try to work the ball down one side of the field only.

3. Encourage players to vary the type, distance, and direction of their passes. Changing the point of attack causes defenders to reposition and possibly create openings in their defense.

4. Attackers dribble at inopportune times or in inappropriate field areas.

4. Constantly remind students that dribbling skills are most effective for one-versus-one situations in the attacking third of the field. Dribbling should be used sparingly in the midfield area and virtually eliminated in the defending third, where one mistake may result in an opponents' score. Emphasize that excessive dribbling, even in the attacking third, serves no purpose and disrupts the teamwork needed to create scoring opportunities.

5. Players fail to support the player with the ball.

5. Successful combination passing only occurs if teammates support one another. Emphasize that support players should position to provide the player with the ball two or three short passing options all of the time. This can only happen if the 10 field players move as a compact unit, that is, supporting one another at the correct distance and angle of support.

6. The team fails to create scoring opportunities with a wide shooting angle to goal.

6. Remind students that the primary offensive objective is to create scoring opportunities front and center of the opponent's goal. Shots from the flank areas provide a narrow angle to goal and are less likely to beat the goalkeeper.

ERROR	CORRECTION
7. Students fail to recognize scoring opportunities, or consistently rely on others to score.	7. Tell your students to be a little selfish near the opponent's goal. A player should not be a ''ball hog,'' but he or she must accept the responsibility of scoring goals. Because in soccer you always miss more shots than you make, players must not fear failure. Encourage students to take a shot if an opportunity arises.

Attacking Principles of Play Drill

1. *Six Versus Four Drill*
[Corresponds to *Soccer*, Step 11]

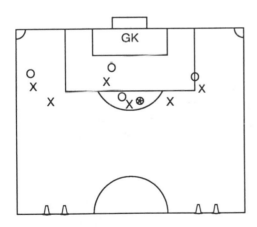

Group Management and Safety Tips

- Play on half of a regulation field.
- Position a regulation-size goal on the endline.
- Position two half-size goals 20 yards apart on the field midline.
- Caution students to play under control at all times. Limit each player to one slide tackle.

Equipment

- Ample supply of soccer balls
- Cones, flags, or similar markers to designate full- and half-size goals
- Scrimmage vests to differentiate teams

Instructions to Class

- ''Six attackers play against four defenders and a goalkeeper in half of the playing field. The six attackers position as three midfielders and three forwards and defend two half-size goals on the field midline. The team of four players and a goalkeeper defend the regulation-size goal.''
- ''The six-player team can score in a variety of ways, each reflecting proper application of one or more principles of attack. Play for 20 minutes. I will keep score and time. I will award points to the 6-player team as follows.''
  a. ''1 point for eight successive passes without loss of possession.''
  b. ''1 point for a successful give and go pass.''
  c. ''1 point for a shot on goal that the goalkeeper saves.''

d. "1 additional point if the shot was from within the width of the penalty area."
e. "2 points for each goal scored from within 18 yards of the goal."
f. "2 points for each goal scored off a cross from the flank."
g. "3 points for beating a defender on the dribble and scoring."
h. "3 points for a goal from 20 yards or greater."

- "I will award points to the team of four as follows."
  a. "1 point for winning ball possession."
  b. "3 points for counterattacking and kicking the ball through either half-size goal."

Student Options

- "Choose from any skills and strategies learned to this point."
- "Each player may perform one slide tackle."

Student Keys to Success (Six-Player Team)

- Use diagonal and checking runs to create additional space and time.
- Position to provide width and depth.
- Create two-versus-one and three-versus-two situations in the field's attacking third.
- Dribble to beat opponents in the attacking third.
- Provide passing options for the player with the ball.
- Create scoring opportunities in central areas, which provide a wider shooting angle to goal.

Team Success Goal

- More points scored than opponents.

To Decrease Difficulty (Six-Player Team)

- Increase goal size.
- Increase field size.
- Reduce opponents to three.

To Increase Difficulty (Six-Player Team)

- Decrease goal size.
- Reduce field size.
- Add an opponent (six versus five).
- Limit players to three touches to receive, pass, or shoot.

Instructor Tally Sheet
Six Versus Four Drill Emphasizing Team Attack

Offensive (Six-Player) Team

Eight passes in succession	_____ × 1 pt	= _____ pts
Successful give and go passes	_____ × 1 pt	= _____ pts
Shots saved by goalkeeper	_____ × 1 pt	= _____ pts
Shots from central location	_____ × 1 pt	= _____ pts
Goals from within 18 yards	_____ × 2 pts	= _____ pts
Goals off crosses from the flank	_____ × 2 pts	= _____ pts
Goals after beating a defender on the dribble	_____ × 3 pts	= _____ pts
Goals from 20+ yards	_____ × 3 pts	= _____ pts
	Total	= _____ pts

Defensive (Four-Player) Team

Wins ball possession by intercepting a pass or tackling successfully	_____ × 1 pt	= _____ pts
Goals scored through half-size goals	_____ × 3 pts	= _____ pts
	Total	= _____ pts

Step 12   Defending as a Team

Strong team defense depends on the physical attributes of each player, the decision-making ability of players in response to constantly changing game situations, and the ability of players to work in combination so that the team defense is greater than the sum of individual abilities.

Physical attributes include quickness, speed, overall body strength, tackling prowess, and heading skill. Students can improve these attributes through dedicated practice. Students can also improve their decision-making abilities by learning more about team defense. Each player must understand his or her role in the framework of team defense. Therefore as instructor you should review the basic principles of team defense with your students. *The principles of team defense* progress sequentially from the moment a team loses ball possession to the instant the team regains it. The principles of defense are universal to all systems of play and should guide individual decision making and behavior. Review these principles from *Soccer: Steps to Success*: applying pressure on the ball, falling back, limiting space in defense, creating defensive depth, denying space behind defense, eliminating passing options, making play predictable, and challenging for the ball.

Error Detection and Correction for Defending as a Team

Physical errors (e.g., a missed tackle or mis-headed ball) occur with inexperienced players and can be corrected through practice of defensive skills under simulated game conditions. Errors in judgment and decision making are generally more difficult to correct. Poor decisions most often result from players' not understanding their roles and responsibilities in team defense. As you observe students in game situations, focus on their decision-making abilities. If students consistently make the wrong decisions, review the principles of team defense (see *Soccer: Steps to Success*) with the entire class to clear up any misunderstandings.

ERROR

CORRECTION

1. The opposing team quickly counterattacks upon gaining ball possession.	1. Emphasize that one or two defenders near the ball must delay the counterattack. They must try to force the opponent to pass backward or square across the field. By delaying the counterattack, defenders gain extra moments to prepare the defense.

ERROR

CORRECTION

2. Defenders away from the ball fail to retreat goalside.

3. Defenders position incorrectly and allow gaps in central areas of the defense.

4. Defenders position flat across the field.

5. Defenders fail to mark opponents near the ball.

2. Encourage students not to be lazy just because they are not near the ball. Players away from the ball should immediately withdraw to a goalside position (between the ball and their goal). From that position they can keep the ball and the opponent they are marking in view.

3. Most goals are scored from central areas, particularly front and center of the goal. Emphasize that defenders must position to control the most vulnerable scoring zones. Attackers will then be forced to shoot from flank areas, where the shooting angle to goal is narrow. Very few goals are scored on shots from the flanks.

4. Defenders must provide cover and balance for one another. Remind students that the first defender marks the dribbler, the second protects the space behind the first, and the third provides balance by positioning diagonally behind the second. Proper positioning of the first, second, and third defenders prevents opponents from penetrating the vulnerable space behind the defense.

5. Have your students memorize the axiom ''The closer an opponent is to the ball, the tighter he or she must be marked.'' Tight marking of opponents near the ball limits the passing options of the player with the ball and increases the likelihood of an attacking error.

Team Defense Drill

Six Versus Four Drill
[Corresponds to *Soccer*, Step 12]

Group Management and Safety Tips
- Play on half of a regulation field.
- Use colored scrimmage vests to differentiate teams.
- Position a regulation-size goal on the endline and two half-size goals 20 yards apart on the midline.
- Caution students to play under control at all times.
- Limit players to one slide tackle.

Equipment
- Ample supply of soccer balls
- Scrimmage vests
- Cones, flags, or similar markers

Instructions to Class
- "This drill emphasizes proper application of the principles of team defense. Six attackers play against four defenders and a goalkeeper. Regular soccer rules apply. The defenders and goalkeeper defend the regulation-size goal while the attackers defend the two half-size goals. Each player may use one slide tackle."
- "The defenders and goalkeeper receive 1 point for tackling successfully or intercepting a pass, or 3 points for counterattacking and scoring through a half-size goal. The six-player team receives 2 points for scoring in the regulation-size goal and 1 point for each shot on goal that the goalkeeper saves. A ball that goes out of bounds is returned with a throw-in. The six-player team gets ball possession to start the game. I will keep time and score. Play for 20 minutes."

Student Options
- "The four-player team can score in either half-size goal."
- "Both teams can use shooting or heading skills to score."

Student Keys to Success (for Defenders)
- Provide cover and balance.
- Restrict space in the most vulnerable scoring zones.
- Limit passing options.
- Force opponents to shoot from flank areas, where the shooting angle is narrow.
- Quickly counterattack upon gaining ball possession.

Team Success Goal
- More points scored than opponents.

To Decrease Difficulty (for Defenders)
- Reduce goal size.
- Reduce playing-area size.
- Limit attackers to three or fewer touches.
- Give defenders another player (a six-versus-five situation).

To Increase Difficulty (for Defenders)
- Increase goal size.
- Increase field size.
- Give attackers another player (a seven-versus-four situation).

Instructor Tally Sheet
Six Versus Four Drill Emphasizing Team Defense

<u>Defensive (Four-player) team</u>

Successful tackles   _____ × 1 pt = _____ pts

Passes intercepted   _____ × 1 pt = _____ pts

Goals scored through half-size goals   _____ × 3 pts = _____ pts

Total = _____ pts

<u>Offensive (Six-player) team</u>

Shots saved by goalkeeper   _____ × 1 pt = _____ pts

Goals scored   _____ × 2 pts = _____ pts

Total = _____ pts

Step 13 Team Organization and Communication

As Steps 11 and 12 stated, players must have a common set of criteria (the principles of attack and defense) to work as a team. Within these criteria students need to know the tactical organization and responsibilities of the field players: They need a system of play. Several systems are used today, and many more have come and gone during soccer's long history. Students must realize from the outset that no magical organization of players can ensure team success. Regardless of the system, players must properly execute basic skills and make correct tactical decisions to achieve a high standard of play. The principles of attack and defense are universal to all systems. What differentiates systems of play are the roles and responsibilities assigned to individual players.

Systems are identified by a series of three numbers: The first refers to the number of defenders, the second to midfielders, and the third to forwards (attackers). (The goalkeeper is not numbered.) For example, among the most popular systems of the modern era are the 4-2-4, 4-4-2, 4-3-3, and 3-5-2. All of these systems deploy at least three defenders, two midfielders, and two forwards. Because a soccer team has 10 field players, the difference between systems results from the roles and responsibilities assigned to the three remaining field players.

Your students know the four systems of play described in *Soccer: Steps to Success*. Emphasize that no one system is necessarily better than any other. What works well for one team might fail miserably for another. The system's worth depends on the nature and ability of the players in the team. You must select a system that highlights player strengths and minimizes their weaknesses.

Error Detection and Correction for Systems of Play

Most errors are generic to all systems. Failure to apply one or more of the principles of attack or defense causes the major problems. As you observe students in games, focus on their decision making and interpretation of their designated role in the team's system of play. Target these aspects of performance in your comments and critical analyses.

ERROR ⃠

CORRECTION

ERROR	CORRECTION
1. The sweeper back fails to cover other defenders.	1. Make sure that students know the sweepers must provide cover for other defenders. The sweeper should be the ''free'' player in defense, assigned to mark no specific opponent.

ERROR 🚫

CORRECTION

2. The stopper back (or marking defender) fails to mark the opposing central forward.

2. The stopper back must be a good one-on-one marker. Remind students that if the stopper allows the opposing center forward to get free the sweeper may be forced to mark the opponent. This will create a lack of defensive cover.

3. A defender tries to dribble out of the field's defending third but loses ball possession.

3. Review the dribbling tactics with your students. Defending players should never take on an opponent in the field's defending third. The risk of error is too great. Teach defenders "safety first" when working the ball out of their defense.

   Remind players that the best method of advancing the ball out of the defending third is interpassing. And a threatened defender can always pass back to the goalkeeper, who then distributes by throwing or kicking.

4. A midfielder consistently loses ball possession through excessive dribbling or poor passing.

4. Midfielders are the vital link between defenders and forwards. They must be creative and contribute to both attack and defense. And most important they must be able to maintain ball possession.

   Coach midfielders to change the point of attack by passing vertically down the field as well as horizontally across the field. Teach midfielders to limit dribbling since it slows play and increases the risk of possession loss.

5. Midfielders play too defensively, failing to attack.

5. Students must not expect forwards to score all goals. Midfielders must occasionally move forward to create scoring opportunities or even finish the attack. They can do so through overlapping runs.

ERROR	CORRECTION
6. The team fails to effectively utilize its midfielders.	6. Defenders sometime bypass midfielders by passing directly to forwards. That may be a good occasional tactic, particularly for a quick counterattack. In most instances, however, defenders should include midfielders in passing combinations to work the ball out of the field's defending third. Involving midfielders in the attack encourages more players to move forward into scoring positions. Then teammates can attack as a compact unit.
7. The front-running forwards are too stationary.	7. To create space for themselves as well as teammates, forwards should move a great deal without the ball. This movement should emphasize checking or diagonal runs to create space. Emphasize to students that a stationary player can be easily marked.
8. The team fails to utilize the field's flank areas.	8. Emphasize width in attack. Players on the flanks must stretch the opponent's defense from touchline to touchline. This tactic forces opponents to cover the greatest possible field area and increases the likelihood of open space in the defense.
9. Front-running players fail to stretch opponents vertically down the field.	9. Have one or two forwards position as targets deep in the opponent's defense. Stretching opponents from front to back destroys defensive cover and may create open space in the defense.
10. Players take poor-percentage shots from the flank areas.	10. Shots from the flanks provide a narrow shooting angle and are therefore easily saved by the goalkeeper. Encourage students to create scoring opportunities with wide shooting angles to goal. The optimal area is front and center of the goal.
11. Forwards pass up scoring opportunities by trying to work the ball very close to goal before shooting.	11. Good scoring opportunities are few and far between. Attackers cannot afford to wait for the perfect shot. Tell your students to prepare to release a shot on goal at a moment's notice.

SIGNALING FOR SUCCESS

The soccer field should not be a quiet place. Communication among teammates should be commonplace because team success depends upon it. Teach your students these guidelines for communicating with teammates.

1. Keep it simple: Make commands clear and concise.
2. Call early: Give teammates sufficient time to respond.
3. Call loudly: Don't be bashful; teammates can't often ask a player to repeat what was said.

Also establish a common set of verbal signals to avoid confusion. Teach students the following commands to use on attack.

1. Call "man-on" or "player-on" when an opponent is directly behind a teammate receiving the ball.
2. Call "turn" when a player has space to turn with the ball and face the opponent's goal.

3. Call "one touch" for a teammate to pass the ball with the first touch.
4. Call "one-two" or "give and go" for a teammate to execute a give and go pass.
5. Call "hold the ball" to warn a teammate to shield the ball from an opponent.
6. Call "dummy it" for a teammate to let the ball roll past to another player.

Teach students the following commands to use when on defense.

1. Call "mark-up" for one-on-one coverage of opponents.
2. Call "close up" for a defender to move closer to the opponent with the ball.
3. Call "weak side" when opponents are advancing on the side of the field away from the ball.
4. Call "runner" when an opponent is running diagonally through the defense.

Team Organization Drill

You need no specific drills or exercises to practice individual systems. But one method of acquainting players with their roles in a system is a shadow drill. Shadow drills simulate player movement in a specific system by using combination passing to move the ball the length of the field. The ball begins in the goalkeeper's hands and ends in the opponent's goal.

Shadow Drill
[Corresponds to *Soccer*, Step 13]

Group Management and Safety Tips
- Organize students into a system of play.
- Play on a regulation-size field with goals.
- Have students execute the drill slowly, usually at half to three-quarters game speed.
- Do not include an opposing team.

Equipment
- Ample supply of soccer balls

Instructions to Class
- "Today we will practice the movement patterns used in the _____ system. Position according to your role in half of the playing field."

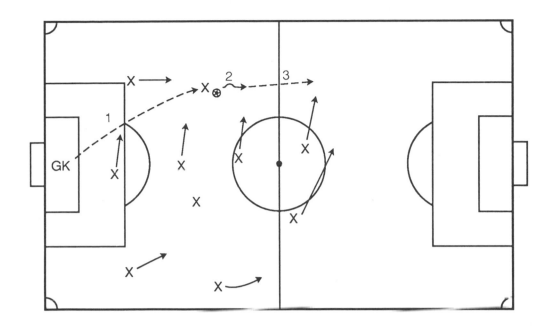

- "The goalkeeper starts each drill repetition by distributing the ball to a defender or midfielder. The field players work as a unit to pass the ball down the field and score in the opposite goal. (We will execute this drill without actual opponents.) Concentrate on proper movement and positioning. Use diagonal and checking runs; provide width, depth, and support in attack; and try to create central scoring opportunities, which provide the widest shooting angle to goal."
- "Play at half game speed."
- "Return to your starting positions after each score. Repeat 20 times."

Student Options

- "The goalkeeper can distribute the ball to any defender or midfielder."
- "The goalkeeper can use any distribution method we have practiced."

Student Keys to Success

- If a defender or midfielder, make yourself available for distribution from the goalkeeper.

- Maintain attack width and depth.
- Use total team support; players should advance as a compact unit.
- Vary the pace, distance, and direction of passes.
- Create scoring opportunities in the most vulnerable scoring zones.
- Finish each attack with a goal.

Student Success Goal

- Correct movement patterns coupled with accurate passes that advance the ball to score in the opposing goal

To Decrease Difficulty

- Slow the drill pace to a fast walk.

To Increase Difficulty

- Execute the drill at game speed.
- Limit all players to three or fewer touches.
- Add six opponents and an opposing goalkeeper, who actively resist the full-sided team's advance.

Evaluation Ideas

Evaluation is the process of determining whether the goals and objectives of your soccer lesson, unit, or entire program are being accomplished. It is an integral part of the educational process. Development of a fair evaluation plan to assess student achievement requires a great deal of thought and planning on your part. Students and teachers alike often perceive evaluation as something that occurs only at the end of a unit or term—a sort of final judgment on the students' overall performance in the class. In reality it should be much more —beginning with the first class period and continuing throughout the term. Ongoing evaluation keeps you informed of individual and group progress and needs, thus providing guidelines for future lesson planning. It also gives students a sense of what they have mastered as well as what they need to improve. Daily assessment of student achievement coupled with appropriate feedback will motivate students to stay up-to-date with new material rather than put things off until later. Final evaluation at the end of the unit will provide you and your students with measures of total student progress and levels of achievement.

Your system of evaluation must reflect the goals and objectives set for the soccer unit. For example, if you expect students to master all of the basic soccer skills; acquire a cognitive understanding of individual, group, and team tactics; and become familiar with basic rules and equipment, then your evaluation plan must provide a fair, reliable, and valid means of assessing progress in all of these areas.

You must provide students with a clear understanding of the goals and objectives of the unit as well as the method of evaluation to be used. Prepare this information in written form and share it with students during the first class period. In doing so you can prevent problems from occurring later in the unit should a student claim that he or she was not properly informed or was confused about how evaluation was to take place.

TESTING PROCEDURES

To successfully play, enjoy, and appreciate soccer, students must master the psychomotor skills used in game situations as well as understand basic tactics and rules. You may monitor student progress in these areas on a regular basis through the use of formative and summative evaluation techniques.

Formative evaluation is an ongoing, day-by-day process that can be used within an individual lesson or class period. Formative evaluation involves direct observation, written tests designed to measure cognitive knowledge, and performance tests that measure physical progress and game skills. Formative evaluation enables students to identify strengths and weaknesses as they progress through the soccer unit. The participant's book, *Soccer: Steps to Success*, provides a system for daily evaluation through the use of the *Keys to Success*, which accompany each skill or tactical situation. The checklists in the keys section can be easily completed by student peers or the teacher to provide an effective means for qualitative (process) assessment of student progress. The *Success Goals*, which accompany each drill or exercise, provide a mechanism for quantitative (product) assessment of student performance. For example, qualitative evaluation of the inside-of-the-foot pass using the Keys to Success would focus on the student's motor execution of the skill. Is the student facing the target; is the balance foot properly positioned; is the kicking foot firmly positioned as it contacts the ball; is the follow-through motion of the kicking leg smooth and fluid? Quantitative evaluation of the same skill using Success Goals would focus on performance results. Using the inside of the foot pass, how many times out of 10 tries can the student pass a stationary ball through a 3-yard wide goal from a distance of 15 yards?

Summative evaluation generally occurs at the completion of an instructional activity or unit to identify overall strengths and weaknesses of students. Summative evaluation should

1. measure individual levels of achievement,
2. compare individuals or groups,
3. establish standards of performance, and
4. provide a basis for establishing a grading system.

Assessment can be accomplished through objective measurements such as knowledge and skill tests, as well as by your subjective judgment of overall student performance. Summative evaluation enables you to identify areas of the soccer unit where students are most deficient and then to provide feedback on how to improve in those areas.

Soccer is difficult to master, particularly in the short time frame of a single term or school year. Successful performance in actual game play requires that players exhibit a high degree of skill proficiency in combination with tactical knowledge and correct decision making. Prior game experience often plays an important role in determining a student's overall level of performance. It is therefore suggested that you combine both outcome (quantitative) and individual technique (qualitative) measures into your system of evaluation. In doing so you will provide students who have little or no experience in the sport with an opportunity to earn A's or passing grades by developing their skills (by following the Keys to Success), even though they may not be accomplished performers in actual game situations. An evaluation system based entirely on performance outcome tends to reward the natural athlete, or those more experienced in the sport, and puts added pressure on the novice who feels pressured to measure up to predetermined standards of performance in an actual game situation.

ADMINISTRATION OF EVALUATION MATERIALS

Much of the ongoing day-by-day evaluation can be accomplished by the students themselves. Whenever possible, have students work in pairs or small groups so they can evaluate one another. The Keys to Success provided in *Soccer: Steps to Success* are particularly suited for peer evaluation. You can also give cognitive quizzes and written tests at selected times throughout the unit to assess students' levels of expertise. Naturally, your daily observations of students as they participate in class activities should also play a role in the final evaluation assessment.

A number of different grading systems can be used for evaluation. These include letter grades (A, B, C, etc.), pass-fail, satisfactory-unsatisfactory, percentages, point systems, plus-minus (−, 0, +), and levels of achievement (gold, silver, bronze), to name a few. Choose the system that best reflects your personal philosophy of grading and how grades should fit into the educational process. Whatever your method of grading, it must be fair and consistent and treat all students in a similar fashion. Your grading system should also take into account special conditions that may affect a student's final evaluation such as illness or injury, physical handicaps, poor attendance, and cheating. To accomplish that aim, you should base final evaluation on a number of different criteria so that no single factor, whether it be a physical test, performance outcome, class attendance, or written test, has too great a weight on a student's overall level of achievement.

Test Bank

This section provides 120 sample questions you can choose from for evaluations. Students should know the answers to these questions after completing a course using *Soccer: Steps to Success*. Select from the questions listed in this Test Bank, choosing those appropriate for your class situation. You may also want to add your own questions. As instructor, you can best decide the appropriate content of your evaluations.

MULTIPLE CHOICE EXAMINATION QUESTIONS

Directions: Choose the answer that *best* completes the question. Select only *one* answer.

_____ 1. The goalkeeper is allowed use of the hands to control the ball within what area?

    a. goal area   c. penalty box
    b. goal box   d. penalty arc

_____ 2. The systems of play described in *Soccer: Steps to Success* deploy at least how many defenders?

    a. two   c. four
    b. three   d. five

_____ 3. A regulation game consists of two equal periods of how many minutes each?

    a. 30 minutes   c. 40 minutes
    b. 50 minutes   d. 45 minutes

_____ 4. What is the circumference and weight of the official FIFA Size #5 soccer ball?

    a. 25 to 26 inches in circumference; 14 to 15 ounces
    b. 27 to 28 inches in circumference; 15 to 16 ounces
    c. 27 to 28 inches in circumference; 14 to 16 ounces
    d. 25 to 27 inches in circumference; 13 to 17 ounces

_____ 5. How is a ball returned into play after it crosses a touchline?

    a. goal kick   c. corner kick
    b. throw-in   d. drop ball

_____ 6. Which of the following violations is *not* a direct foul?

    a. holding an opponent   c. tripping an opponent
    b. obstructing an opponent   d. propelling the ball with hand or arm

_____ 7. What organization is the international governing body of soccer?

    a. USSF   c. FIFA
    b. USYSA   d. NCAA

_____ 8. What is the most basic technique used to pass the ball over distances of 15 or fewer yards?

    a. instep pass   c. outside-of-the-foot pass
    b. inside-of-the-foot pass   d. side-volley pass

_____ 9. Which would be the most appropriate foot surface for receiving a rolling ball when under pressure of an opponent?

    a. outside   c. inside
    b. sole   d. instep

_____ 10. Which of the following is *not* correct form when executing a short chip pass?
   a. approaching the ball from a slight angle
   b. squaring shoulders with the intended target
   c. using a long, sweeping follow-through of the kicking leg
   d. contacting the ball's lower edge with the instep

_____ 11. Dribbling skills can be used to best advantage in which field section?
   a. defending third
   b. midfield third
   c. attacking third
   d. any field section

_____ 12. Which of the following is *not* correct form when dribbling for speed?
   a. maintaining an upright posture
   b. keeping head up and vision on the field as much as possible
   c. contacting ball with instep or outside surface of the foot
   d. keeping the ball in close control of feet at all times

_____ 13. How should you position your body when shielding the ball from an opponent?
   a. Stand with your back to the opponent.
   b. Stand sideways to the opponent with the ball between your feet.
   c. Stand sideways to the opponent and control the ball with the foot farthest from the opponent.
   d. None of the above.

_____ 14. Which type of tackle is preferred in most situations?
   a. block tackle
   b. poke tackle
   c. slide tackle
   d. two-footed tackle

_____ 15. The proper defensive stance has feet positioned in what manner?
   a. square to one another with weight centered over balls of feet
   b. staggered (one foot slightly ahead of the other) with weight back on heels
   c. square to one another with weight back on heels
   d. staggered (one foot slightly ahead of the other) with weight centered over balls of feet

_____ 16. Which of the following is *not* correct form when jumping to head a ball?
   a. jump early
   b. use a one-footed takeoff
   c. arch the upper body back
   d. contact the ball on the flat surface of the forehead

_____ 17. What is the most common technique used to shoot a stationary or rolling ball?
   a. instep drive
   b. full volley
   c. half volley
   d. side volley

_____ 18. Which technique is used to shoot a ball directly out of the air?
   a. instep drive
   b. full volley
   c. half volley
   d. swerving shot

_____ 19. How should the goalkeeper position his or her hands when in the "ready position"?
   a. hands at chest level with palms forward and fingers pointed down
   b. hands at waist level with palms forward and fingers pointed down
   c. hands at shoulder level with palms forward and fingers pointed up
   d. hands at waist level with palms forward and fingers pointed up

_____ 20. How should a goalkeeper receive a ball rolling directly at him or her?

    a. kneel on one knee and allow the ball to roll up onto forearms

    b. stand erect with legs together, bend forward at waist, and catch the ball in palms

    c. stand erect with legs together, bend forward at waist, and allow the ball to roll up onto forearms

    d. drop to both knees and catch ball in palms

_____ 21. Defensive cover is usually provided by which defender?

    a. first defender   c. third defender

    b. second defender   d. fourth defender

_____ 22. In a 4-2-4 system of play, the number 2 represents which of the field players?

    a. defenders   c. strikers

    b. midfielders   d. wingers

_____ 23. Which of the following is not a principle of team attack?

    a. player movement with and without the ball

    b. concentrating players in central areas of the field

    c. improvising: dribbling at opportune times

    d. total team support

_____ 24. Which of the following is *not* true about the dimensions of a regulation soccer field?

    a. length may vary between 100 and 130 yards

    b. width may vary between 40 and 80 yards

    c. field must be rectangular

    d. field must be marked by distinctive lines no more than 5 inches wide

_____ 25. What is the size of a regulation soccer goal?

    a. 8 feet high by 16 feet wide

    b. 8 yards high by 24 yards wide

    c. 8 feet high by 24 feet wide

    d. 8 feet high by 6 yards wide

_____ 26. How far is the penalty spot from the goal line?

    a. 8 yards   c. 12 yards

    b. 10 yards   d. 14 yards

_____ 27. How should the referee restart play if unsure of who last touched an out-of-bounds ball?

    a. flip a coin and award a kick-in to the team that wins the toss

    b. flip a coin and award a throw-in to the team that wins the toss

    c. perform a drop ball at the spot where the ball was last in bounds

    d. award a throw-in to the team that is behind in score

_____ 28. A ball that passes over the goal line (excluding the portion between the goal posts) and was last touched by a defender is returned to play by which of the following?

    a. goal kick   c. indirect free kick

    b. corner kick   d. goalkeeper punt

_____ 29. In which of the following is the ball *not* considered out of play?

    a. ball travels over the goal line

    b. ball rebounds off the referee within the field

    c. ball travels over a touchline

    d. referee stops the action due to an injury

_____ 30. The clock is stopped for which of the following?
   a. a drop ball   c. an indirect free kick
   b. a corner kick   d. a penalty kick

MATCHING EXAMINATION QUESTIONS

Directions: Match the term with its *best* definition.

_____ 1. ball watching   _____ 19. full volley
_____ 2. cover   _____ 20. USYSA
_____ 3. direct free kick   _____ 21. warm-up
_____ 4. economical training   _____ 22. shielding
_____ 5. far post   _____ 23. midfielder
_____ 6. goal-side position   _____ 24. one-touch soccer
_____ 7. functional training   _____ 25. offside
_____ 8. near post   _____ 26. tripping
_____ 9. balance   _____ 27. ready position
_____ 10. overlap   _____ 28. feints
_____ 11. restarts   _____ 29. dummy
_____ 12. sweeper   _____ 30. poke tackle
_____ 13. stopper   _____ 31. checking run
_____ 14. touchline   _____ 32. dive header
_____ 15. cool-down   _____ 33. W position
_____ 16. wall pass   _____ 34. javelin throw
_____ 17. half volley   _____ 35. striker
_____ 18. penalty shot

a.   the "free" player in defense who covers the marking defenders
b.   positioning between the ball and an opponent attempting to gain possession
c.   a tactic used to move defenders and midfielders into attacking positions
d.   side boundary of the field
e.   player focuses solely on the ball and loses sight of the opponent he or she is supposed to mark
f.   positioning defenders away from the ball to protect the vital space behind the defense
g.   a method of goalkeeper distribution used to distribute the ball over short distances
h.   give and go pass
i.   defensive support
j.   body movements designed to unbalance an opponent
k.   a training regimen that makes optimal use of available practice time
l.   exercises that warm the muscles and prepare the body for vigorous activity
m.   the result of a direct foul committed by a defender within his or her penalty area
n.   a central marking defender
o.   goal kicks, corner kicks, free kicks, and drop balls
p.   the goalkeeper's basic stance when the ball enters shooting range
q.   a situation in which an attacker positioned in the opponents' half of the field does not have two opponents between him- or herself and the goal at the moment the ball is played to him or her
r.   striking a dropping ball at the moment it hits ground
s.   a front-running central attacker
t.   United States Soccer Federation
u.   acrobatic skill used to score goals off low crosses in the goal area

v.   the goalpost more distant from the ball position
w.   interpassing among teammates without stopping the ball
x.   an affiliate of the USSF
y.   shooting a ball directly out of the air
z.   a player who links the defenders with the attackers and contributes to both attack and defense
aa.   the goal post closer to the ball position
bb.   movement used to create space between the player with the ball and the marking opponent
cc.   method of goalkeeper distribution used to distribute the ball over distances of 40 or more yards
dd.   one of nine offenses warranting a direct foul
ee.   a restart situation that can be scored directly by the shooter
ff.   correct position of a defender when marking an opponent
gg.   method of tackling in which a player slides and kicks the ball away from an opponent
hh.   position of the goalkeeper's hands when fielding a chest-high ball
ii.   method of tackling in which a player extends his or her leg and kicks the ball away from an opponent
jj.   the preferred method of tackling the ball away from an opponent
kk.   legal tactic to challenge an opponent for the ball when the ball is in playing distance
ll.   isolating the skills and tactics of a specific playing position
mm. the portion of practice devoted to stretching muscles and returning body functions to their normal state
nn.   stepping over the ball and letting it roll past you to a teammate

TRUE/FALSE EXAMINATION QUESTIONS

Directions: Mark a T (true) or F (false) in the space next to the question. Any statement not clearly marked T or F will be counted incorrect.

_____ 1. The center circle has a 10-foot radius.
_____ 2. The penalty area is contained within the goal area.
_____ 3. A goal cannot be scored directly off a goal kick.
_____ 4. A player cannot be offside if positioned within his or her team's half of the field.
_____ 5. Charging an opponent with your shoulder when the ball is not in playing distance is a direct foul.
_____ 6. The goalkeeper is permitted to take six steps with ball possession before releasing it to a teammate.
_____ 7. A player ejected from a game cannot return and cannot be replaced by a substitute.
_____ 8. Opposing players must position at least 5 yards from the ball when a player takes a direct free kick.
_____ 9. The inside and outside surfaces of the foot are used primarily to pass and receive ground balls.
_____ 10. When executing the inside-of-the-foot pass, the balance foot should be planted behind and to the side of the ball.
_____ 11. Only minimal follow through of the kicking leg should be used for the short chip pass.
_____ 12. When receiving a lofted ball with your instep, you should angle your foot diagonally upward so that the ball bounces back into your body.
_____ 13. You should use the inside surface of your foot to push the ball forward when dribbling for speed in open space.

_____ 14. You should contact the ball along your hairline when executing the jump header.

_____ 15. You should use a two-footed takeoff when jumping up to head the ball.

_____ 16. The principles of defense differ for a 4-2-4 system of play and a 2-3-5 system of play.

_____ 17. For the instep-drive shot, the knee of the kicking leg should be over the ball at the moment the foot contacts it.

_____ 18. The goalkeeper should attempt to catch a hard, low shot in his or her palms.

_____ 19. The goalkeeper should use a two-footed takeoff when jumping up to catch a high ball.

_____ 20. The goalkeeper should land on his or her side when diving to save a shot.

_____ 21. Players should generally position at narrow angles of support.

_____ 22. The second defender's primary responsibility is to protect the vital space behind the defense on the side of the field opposite the ball.

_____ 23. On the average, the typical soccer player has ball possession for about 12 minutes of a 90-minute match.

_____ 24. Players should limit dribbling in their defending third of the field.

_____ 25. The sweeper and stopper backs should never cross the field midline.

_____ 26. When describing a system of play, the first number refers to the forwards, the second to the midfielders, and the third to the defenders.

_____ 27. During a regulation game the clock stops after a goal has been scored and when the ball travels over a touchline or endline.

_____ 28. When taking a throw-in a player must face the field, hold the ball in both hands, and deliver it from behind and over his or her head.

_____ 29. A player cannot be offside directly from a corner kick.

_____ 30. A player in an offside position should always be penalized for being offside.

FILL IN-THE-BLANK EXAMINATION QUESTIONS

Directions: From the following list of terms, fill in the blanks with the word, phrase, or number that best completes the statement.

Word/Phrase List

overlap	four	FIFA
checking	five	USYSA
diagonal	six	side of head
yellow	javelin	top of head
red	baseball	forehead
green	drop ball	left
square	touchlines	right
staggered	endlines	one versus one
block	penalty spot	1994
poke	W	eight
slide	HEH	direct
instep drive	give-and-go	hairline
full volley	narrow	1996
goal kick	wide	two versus two
corner kick	110	10
placekick	120	12
inside-of-the-foot	130	indirect
outside of the foot	USSF	penalty arc

1. Tripping is a foul penalized by awarding a(n) _____ free kick to the team of the player who was fouled.
2. The penalty spot is _____ yards front and center of the goal.
3. The referee will hold up a(n) _____ card to signal that a player has been ejected from the game.
4. A type of running pattern in which a defender moves forward past a midfielder or forward is called a(n) _____ run.
5. You can use a(n) _____ run to create space between yourself and the opponent marking you.
6. The most basic type of pass in soccer is the _____ pass.
7. The goalkeeper is allowed _____ steps with ball possession before releasing it to another player.
8. The goalkeeper should use the _____ throw to toss the ball 40 yards or farther.
9. When dribbling for speed, you should use the _____ to push the ball forward.
10. The _____ tackle should be used only as a last resort when another type of tackle is not possible.
11. The most basic tactical unit is the _____.
12. The proper defensive posture has feet placed in a(n) _____ stance.
13. If the referee whistles a stoppage of play due to the ball's hitting a dog that wandered onto the field, play should be restarted with a(n) _____ at the point where the ball was blown dead.
14. The most basic technique used to shoot a rolling or stationary ball is the _____.
15. A ball that goes over the endline and was last touched by a defender is returned to play by a(n) _____.
16. The goalkeeper's hand position, with fingers spread and thumbs almost touching, is generally referred to as the _____.
17. The most effective method of beating a single defender in a two-versus-one situation is the _____ pass.
18. Teammates should position to form a(n) _____ angle of support for the player with the ball.
19. The side boundaries of the field are referred to as the _____.
20. The _____ has a radius of 10 yards from the penalty spot and is drawn outside of the penalty area.
21. The maximum allowable length of a soccer field is _____ yards.
22. The _____ administers and promotes soccer in the United States for players under 19 years.
23. When executing the dive header a player should contact the ball on the _____.
24. The United States will host the World Cup Tournament in _____.
25. When playing as a goalkeeper you should push off with your _____ foot when diving to your right to make a save.

WRITTEN EXAMINATION ANSWERS

Multiple Choice	Matching	True/False	Fill-In-the-Blank
1. c	1. e	1. F	1. direct
2. b	2. i	2. F	2. 12
3. d	3. ee	3. T	3. red
4. c	4. k	4. T	4. overlap
5. b	5. v	5. F	5. checking
6. b	6. ff	6. F	6. inside-of-the-foot
7. c	7. ll	7. T	7. four
8. b	8. aa	8. F	8. javelin
9. a	9. f	9. T	9. outside of the foot
10. c	10. c	10. F	10. slide
11. c	11. o	11. T	11. one versus one
12. d	12. a	12. F	12. staggered
13. c	13. n	13. F	13. drop ball
14. a	14. d	14. F	14. instep drive
15. d	15. mm	15. T	15. corner kick
16. b	16. h	16. F	16. W
17. a	17. r	17. T	17. give-and-go
18. b	18. m	18. F	18. wide
19. d	19. y	19. F	19. touchlines
20. c	20. x	20. T	20. penalty arc
21. b	21. l	21. F	21. 130
22. b	22. b	22. F	22. USYSA
23. b	23. z	23. F	23. forehead
24. b	24. w	24. T	24. 1994
25. c	25. q	25. F	25. right
26. c	26. dd	26. F	
27. c	27. p	27. F	
28. b	28. j	28. T	
29. b	29. nn	29. T	
30. d	30. ii	30. F	
	31. bb		
	32. u		
	33. hh		
	34. cc		
	35. s		

Appendices

Appendix A
How to Use the Knowledge Structure Overview

A knowledge structure is a valuable instructional tool for teachers and coaches alike. Your personal knowledge structure outlines what you know about soccer and how you organize that knowledge from a teaching or coaching perspective. The knowledge structure provided in this text targets primarily a teaching and learning environment. It emphasizes the development of skills and tactics rather than physiological and conditioning factors. In a competitive sport environment where physiological concerns are equally important, you can adjust the training progressions to accommodate the fitness and conditioning needs of athletes.

The Knowledge Structure of Soccer shows the first page, or an overview, of a completed knowledge structure and is divided into four subcategories of information. These categories are the starting point for all of the participant books and instructor guides in the Steps to Success Activity Series:

- Physiological training and conditioning
- Background knowledge
- Psychomotor skills and strategies
- Psychosocial concepts

Physiological training and conditioning here consist of warm-up and cool-down. Research in exercise physiology and medicine has substantiated the importance of a warm-up before and a cool-down after practice. The participant book and the instructor guide each provide principles and exercises for effective clapsychos warm-up and cool-down. A more competitive sport environment would also mandate sessions on training principles, injury prevention, training progressions, and nutritional needs.

The background-knowledge category presents subcategories of information essential to all soccer instructors and coaches. Soccer background knowledge includes playing the game, basic rules of play/safety, soccer today, and equipment.

Individual skills, as well as individual, small-group, and team tactics, appear under the category of psychomotor skills/strategies. For soccer, the basic skills include passing and receiving ground and lofted balls, dribbling, tackling, heading, shooting, and goalkeeping. These skills appear in a recommended instructional order. In a complete knowledge structure, each skill is broken down into subskills with biomechanical, motor learning, and other teaching and coaching points that exemplify mature performance. These points appear in the Keys to Success for each skill in the participant book.

Once individual skills are identified and analyzed, basic tactics, or strategies, are also identified and analyzed. Tactics involve decision making and sometimes combination play among teammates. For soccer, the strategies include individual, small group, and team tactics of attack and defense; and team organization (systems of play).

The psychosocial category identifies psychological and social concepts proven to contribute to learners' understanding of and success in the activity. These concepts are built into the key concepts and activities for teaching. For soccer the concepts include anticipation, preparation, analyzation, and reaction—all aspects of reading the game.

To be a successful teacher or coach you must not only possess a comprehensive base of knowledge but also effectively convey what you know to others. A knowledge structure will help you organize your thoughts and ideas in a clear and precise progression. Your knowledge structure is the most basic level of teaching knowledge you possess for a sport or activity. For more information on developing your own knowledge structure, see the textbook that accompanies this series, *Instructional Design for Teaching Physical Activities* (Vickers, 1990).

Knowledge Structure of Soccer (Overview)

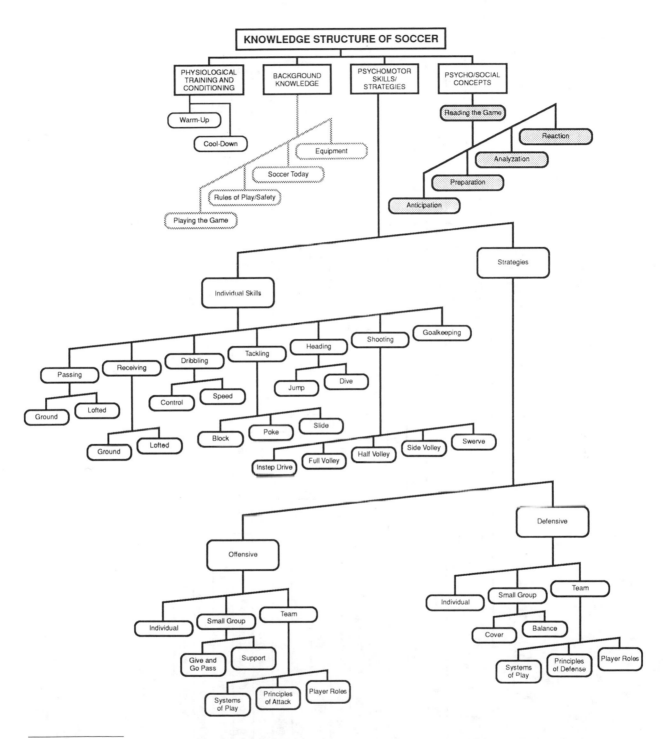

Note. From ''The Role of Expert Knowledge Structures in an Instructional Design Model for Physical Education'' by J.N. Vickers, 1983, *Journal of Teaching in Physical Education,* **2**(3), 25, 27. Copyright 1983 by Joan N. Vickers. Adapted by permission. This Knowledge Structure of Soccer was designed specifically for the Steps to Success Activity Series by Joan N. Vickers and Joseph A. Luxbacher.

Appendix B.1

Sample Scope and Teaching Sequence

New [N]   Review [R]   Continue [C]

Name of activity: Soccer
Level of learner: Beginner

Steps	Session Number →	1	2	3	4	5	6	7	8	9	10	11	12	13	14	15	16	17	18	19	20	21	22	23	24	25	26	27	28	29	30
1	Passing and receiving ground balls	N	R	C	C	C	C	C	C	C	C	C	C	C	C	C	C	C	C	C	C	C	C	C	C	C	C	C	C	C	C
2	Passing and receiving lofted balls			N	R	C	C	C	C	C	C	C	C	C	C	C	C	C	C	C	C	C	C	C	C	C	C	C	C	C	C
3	Individual ball possession						N	R	C	C	C	C	C	C	C	C	C	C	C	C	C	C	C	C	C	C	C	C	C	C	C
4	Gaining possession of the ball									N	R	C	C	C	C	C	C	C	C	C	C	C	C	C	C	C	C	C	C	C	C
5	Individual attack and defense tactics												N	R	C	C	C	C	C	C	C	C	C	C	C	C	C	C	C	C	C
6	Heading skills															N	R	C	C	C	C	C	C	C	C	C	C	C	C	C	C
7	Shooting skills																N	R	C	C	C	C	C	C	C	C	C	C	C	C	C
8	Goalkeeping																			N	R	C	C	C	C	C	C	C	C	C	C
9	Small group strategies in attack																						N	R	C	C	C	C	C	C	C
10	Small group strategies in defense																							N	R	C	C	C	C	C	C
11	Attacking as a team																								N	R	C	C	C	C	C
12	Defending as a team																										N	R	C	C	C
13	Team organization and communication																													N	R

Note. Form from *Badminton: A Structures of Knowledge Approach* (p. 60, 61) by J.N. Vickers and D. Brecht, 1987, Calgary, AB: University Printing Services. Copyright 1987 by Joan N. Vickers. Adapted by permission.

Appendix B.2
How to Use the Scope and Teaching Sequence Form

Consider your completed scope and teaching sequence a master lesson plan. It lists all the skills and tactics to be included in your course, recorded (vertically) in the progressive sequence you have decided to present them and showing (horizontally) the manner and the sessions in which you will teach them.

The Sample Scope and Teaching Sequence for Soccer (Appendix B.1) illustrates how to use the chart. When read vertically, this chart indicates, for example that in session 8 the students will continue (C) working on the passing, receiving, and dribbling skills presented in Steps 1, 2, and 3. These skills are used primarily to maintain ball possession and to advance the ball into the opponent's end of the field. Also in session 8 the defensive skills of tackling are introduced as a new topic (N). When read horizontally, the Sample Scope and Teaching Sequence for Soccer also indicates, for example, that the skills in Step 3 are practiced for 20 sessions—one introductory session, one review session, and 18 sessions of continuations.

Use the blank form in Appendix B.2 to prepare a scope and teaching sequence for your class situation. This sequence will help you plan your daily teaching strategies (see the Lesson Plan Form in Appendix D.2) and structure your overall course plan. Initially you may find it difficult to accurately predict how much material you can cover in each class session. But by completing a scope and teaching sequence you can compare your actual progress to the plan and adjust the plan to better accommodate the next class.

The scope and teaching sequence will also help you organize the course material to best fit the class time available. In the sample, all of the skills and tactics are covered in 30 sessions. However, as instructor, you must be flexible to your students' needs and abilities. Experienced students could cover the required material in less time while beginners may need more. If you do not have 30 sessions to devote to your soccer unit you may want to focus your instruction on skill development, planning to cover tactics in later units or in subsequent years. When planning your course's scope and teaching sequence, also remember to allot ample time for reviewing and practicing each skill or tactical concept, and for testing and evaluation.

Appendix B.2 (Continued)

Scope and Teaching Sequence

NAME OF ACTIVITY _____

LEVEL OF LEARNER _____

New **N**   Review **R**   Continue **C**

Steps	Session Number	1	2	3	4	5	6	7	8	9	10	11	12	13	14	15	16	17	18	19	20	21	22	23	24	25	26	27	28	29	30
1																																
2																																
3																																
4																																
5																																
6																																
7																																
8																																
9																																
10																																
11																																
12																																
13																																
14																																
15																																
16																																
17																																
18																																
19																																
20																																
21																																
22																																
23																																
24																																
25																																

Note. From _Badminton: A Structures of Knowledge Approach_ (pp. 60, 61) by J.N. Vickers and D. Brecht, 1987, Calgary, AB: University Printing Services. Copyright 1987 by Joan N. Vickers. Adapted by permission.

Appendix C.1

Sample Individual Program

INDIVIDUAL COURSE IN _____ GRADE/COURSE SECTION _____

STUDENT'S NAME _____ STUDENT ID # _____

I. PHYSICAL SKILLS	TECHNIQUE AND PERFORMANCE OBJECTIVES	WT* X	POINT PROGRESS**				= FINAL SCORE***
			1	2	3	4	
1 Passing Ground Balls	Technique: Number out of 10 trials student demonstrates 80% or more of items on checklists for inside-of-the-foot, outside-of-the-foot and instep passes.		5	6	7	8+	
	Performance: Number out of 10 trials ball passed between two cones 3 yards apart from 15 yards away.	7%	5	6	7	8+	
2 Receiving Ground Balls	Technique: Number out of 10 trials student demonstrates 80% or more of items on checklists for inside- and outside-of-the-foot techniques.		5	6	7	8+	
	Performance: Number out of 10 trials ball received and controlled with appropriate foot surface.	7%	5	6	7	8+	
3 Passing Lofted Balls	Technique: Number out of 10 trials student demonstrates 80% or more of items on checklists for short- and long-chip passes		5	6	7	8+	
	Performance: Number out of 10 trials ball chipped into circle 5 yards in diameter from 15 yards away.	7%	5	6	7	8+	
4 Receiving Lofted Balls	Technique: Number out of 10 trials student demonstrates 80% or more of items on checklists for instep, thigh, chest, and head receiving techniques.		5	6	7	8+	
	Performance: Number out of 10 trials ball received and controlled with appropriate body surface.	7%	5	6	7	8+	
5 Dribbling	Technique: Number out of 10 trials student demonstrates 80% or more of items on checklists for dribbling for close control and dribbling for speed.		5	6	7	8+	
	Performance: Number out of 10 trials that student dribbles slalom course without knocking down any cones. Slalom course consists of 8 cones spaced 2 yards apart in straight line.	6%	5	6	7	8+	

(Cont.)

Sample Individual Program (Cont.)

#	Skill	Description	%					
6	Heading	*Technique:* Number out of 10 trials student demonstrates 80% or more of items on checklists for jump- and dive-header techniques.		5	6	7	8+	
		Performance: Number out of 10 trials that student heads tossed ball directly to chest of partner standing 5 yards away.	5%	5	6	7	8+	
7	Shooting	*Technique:* Number out of 10 trials student demonstrates 80% or more of items on checklists for instep drive, full volley, half volley, side volley, and swerve shots.		5	6	7	8+	
		Performance: Number out of 10 trials that student shoots stationary ball into open goal from 22 yards away.	6%	5	6	7	8+	
8	Goalkeeping	*Technique:* Number out of 10 trials student demonstrates 80% or more of items on checklists for goalkeeping.		5	6	7	8+	
		Performance: Number out of 10 trials that student catches ball kicked straight on from 10 yards away. Student must use W position of hands for any ball above chest height.	5%	5	6	7	8+	

Subtotal Physical Skills = 50%

II. COGNITIVE CONCEPTS

#	Concept	Description	%				
1	Individual Tactics	*Performance:* Percentage of correct answers to quiz on individual attack and defense tactics.	5%				
2	Small Group Attack and Defense Tactics	*Performance:* Percentage of correct answers to quiz on small group tactics of attack and defense (e.g., give and go pass, support, cover, balance).	5%				
3	Team Attack and Defense Tactics	*Performance:* Percentage of correct answers to quiz on team tactics of attack and defense.	5%				
4	Systems of Play	*Performance:* Percentage of correct answers to quiz on various modern systems of play.	5%				
5	Culminating Knowledge Test	*Performance:* Percentage of correct answers on final examination.	30%				

Subtotal Cognitive = 50%

Total = 100%

Note. Form from "The Role of Expert Knowledge Structures in an Instructional Design Model for Physical Education" by J.N. Vickers, 1983, *Journal of Teaching in Physical Education,* 2(3), p. 17. Copyright 1983 by Joan N. Vickers. Adapted by permission.

*WT = Weighting of an objective's degree of difficulty.

**PROGRESS = Ongoing success, which may be expressed in terms of (a) accumulated points (1, 2, 3, 4); (b) grades (D, C, B, A); (c) symbols (merit, bronze, silver, gold); (d) unsatisfactory/satisfactory; and others as desired.

***FINAL SCORE equals WT times PROGRESS.

Appendix C.2
How to Use the Individual Program Form

To complete an individual program for each student in your class you must first make five decisions about evaluation:

1. How many skills or concepts should you evaluate? Consider the number of students and the time available: The larger the class size and the shorter the class length, the fewer skills and concepts you can use.
2. What quantitative or qualitative criteria will you use for evaluation? See the Sample Individual Program (Appendix C.1) for ideas.
3. What relative weight should each skill or tactical concept receive? To make this decision you should consider the skill or tactic's overall importance in the course and the amount of practice time provided to learn it.
4. What type of grading system will you use? Choose from letter grades (A, B, C, D), pass/fail, satisfactory/unsatisfactory, percentages (90%, 80%, 70%, etc.), and plus/minus (−, 0, ┼). Inform students of your grading system during the first class.
5. Who will do the evaluating? If the class is very large you may need help in evaluating. For instance, you could delegate specific quantitative evalua-

tions to students' peers, but leave all qualitative evaluations and final-grade determinations to you.

Once you have finalized your decisions about student evaluation, prepare an evaluation sheet (using the blank form in Appendix C.2) appropriate for most of your students. Calculate the minimum passing and maximum attainable scores, and then create as many grade categories as you wish within that range.

The blank Individual Program provides ideas that you can adapt to integrate into your own teaching situation. It is not intended to be used exactly as it appears, though you may do so if you wish.

Give each student in your class a copy of the program evaluation system during the first class. Be prepared to adapt the program for students who need special consideration. Program modifications could include changing the weight assigned to specific skills or tactical concepts, or varying the criteria used for evaluating those students. However you do so, you must recognize and effectively deal with individual differences among your students. As instructor you must also remember that not all students have the potential to become excellent players, and so that should not be a primary requisite for passing the course.

Appendix C.2 (Continued)

Individual Program

INDIVIDUAL COURSE IN _____ GRADE/COURSE SECTION _____

STUDENT'S NAME _____ STUDENT ID # _____

SKILLS/CONCEPTS	TECHNIQUE AND PERFORMANCE OBJECTIVES	WT* ×	POINT PROGRESS**				= FINAL SCORE***
			1	2	3	4	

Note. From "The Role of Expert Knowledge Structures in an Instructional Design Model for Physical Education" by J.N. Vickers, 1983, *Journal of Teaching in Physical Education*, 2(3), p. 17. Copyright 1983 by Joan N. Vickers. Adapted by permission.

*WT = Weighting of an objective's degree of difficulty.

**PROGRESS = Ongoing success, which may be expressed in terms of (a accumulated points (1, 2, 3, 4); (b) grades (D, C, B, A); (c) symbols (merit, bronze, silver, gold); (d) unsatisfactory/satisfactory; and others as desired.

***FINAL SCORE equals WT times PROGRESS.

Appendix D.1
Sample Lesson Plan

Lesson plan _____2_____ of _____30_____ Activity _____Soccer_____

Class _____ 1:00-2:05

Equipment:

- Soccer balls
- Cones
- Scrimmage vests

Objectives: By completion of the class each student will be able to perform the following:

1. Use inside of foot to pass and receive rolling ball with stationary partner 10 yards away accurately and with control 17 of 20 times.
2. Use outside of foot to pass and receive rolling ball with stationary partner 10 yards away accurately and with control 15 of 20 times.
3. Use instep of foot to pass and outside of foot to receive rolling ball with stationary partner 25 yards away accurately and with control 14 of 20 times.
4. Use inside, outside, or instep of foot while circulating through a 15-by-25-yard grid, to pass and receive a rolling ball with two or more classmates accurately and with control for 5 minutes.
5. Use inside, outside, or instep of foot to work with two classmates to maintain ball possession for eight or more consecutive passes from challenging opponent in a 15-by-15-yard area.

Skill or concept	Learning activity	Teaching points	Time (min)
1. Outline objectives	• See above.	• See above.	5
2. Warm up	• Jog randomly, dribbling a ball for close control. • Perform flexibility and agility exercises.	• When dribbling keep head up for good field vision. • Don't bounce when stretching; use static stretch.	5
3. Passing and receiving with inside of foot	• Divide students into pairs. Have students kick ball back and forth with partner, using inside of foot to pass and receive. • Limit students to two touches, one to receive and control and one to return ball to partner.	• Withdraw foot to absorb ball impact. • Firmly position foot when passing. • Square shoulders with target when passing. • Strike ball through center with inside surface of foot.	10

Skill or concept	Learning activity	Teaching points	Time (min)
4. Passing and receiving with outside of foot	• Divide students into pairs. Have students kick ball back and forth with partner, using outside of foot to pass and receive. • Limit students to two touches, one to receive and control and one to return ball to partner.	• When receiving, position sideways and receive ball on outside surface of instep. • Withdraw receiving foot to absorb ball impact. • When passing, angle kicking foot down and in, and keep it firmly positioned. • Use inside-out kicking motion to pass ball.	10
5. Passing with instep and receiving with outside of foot	• Divide students into pairs. Have students kick ball back and forth with partner, using instep of foot to pass and outside of foot to receive ball. • Limit students to two touches, one to receive and control and one to return ball to partner.	• Firmly position kicking foot with toes pointed down when passing. • Strike ball directly through vertical midline. • Position body sideways when receiving, with receiving foot angled down and in. • Withdraw receiving foot to cushion ball impact.	10
6. Passing and receiving rolling ball with two or more classmates while jogging in designated area	• Organize students into groups of three. Position each group in a 15-by-25-yard grid. • Have students pass and receive ball among themselves while jogging randomly in grid.	• Pass and receive ball in fluid manner. • Correct timing and pace of passes. • Receive ball in range of control. • Receive ball into open space.	10

(Cont.)

Skill or concept	Learning activity	Teaching points	Time (min)
7. Three students using combination passing to maintain ball possession from opponent in a 15-by-15-yard grid	• Organize students into groups of four. Designate one as defender and three as attackers. • Attackers use passing combinations to maintain ball possession from the defender in grid.	• Attackers use width and length of grid when passing to unbalance defender. • Attackers use one- and two-touch passing whenever possible.	10
8. Closing	• Review major points of lesson. • Provide performance-related feedback. • Provide objectives for next lesson. • Cool down and stretch.	• Have students stretch each major muscle group used during class.	5

Note. Form from *Badminton: A Structures of Knowledge Approach* (p. 95) by J.N. Vickers and D. Brecht, 1987, Calgary, AB: University Printing Services. Copyright 1987 by Joan N. Vickers. Adapted by permission.

Appendix D.2
How to Use the Lesson Plan Form

In their training all teachers learn that lesson plans are vital to good teaching. This is a commonly accepted axiom, but lesson plans can take a variety of forms.

Whatever the form, an effective lesson plan sets forth objectives to be attained or attempted during the session. Without objectives, teaching is pointless and no basis exists for judging teaching effectiveness.

Once you name your objectives, list specific activities that lead to attaining each. Describe every activity in detail. What will take place and in what order, and how class organization will optimize learning situations. Record key words or phrases as focal points and reminders of applicable safety precautions.

Finally, to guide you in keeping to your plan, set a time schedule that allocates a segment of the lesson for each activity. Also include in your lesson plan a list of all necessary equipment; this list will remind you to check for the equipment availability and location before class.

An organized, professional approach to teaching requires daily lesson plans. Each lesson plan provides you an effective overview of your intended instruction and a means to evaluate it when class is over. Having lesson plans on file also allows someone else to teach in your absence and offers some protection in liability suits.

You may modify the blank lesson plan here to fit your own needs. You might also add on the back student practice options and ways to decrease or increase the difficulty of the tasks you have planned.

Lesson Plan

LESSON PLAN _____ OF _____	OBJECTIVES:
ACTIVITY _____	
CLASS _____	

SKILL OR CONCEPT	LEARNING ACTIVITIES	TEACHING POINTS	TIME

Note. From *Badminton: A Structures of Knowledge Approach* (p. 95) by J.N. Vickers and D. Brecht, 1987, Calgary, AB: University Printing Services. Copyright 1987 by Joan N. Vickers. Reprinted by permission.

References

Goc-Karp, G., & Zakrajsek, D.B. (1987). Planning for learning: Theory into practice. *Journal of Teaching in Physical Education,* **6**(4), 377-392.

Housner, L.D., & Griffey, D.C. (1985). Teacher cognition: Differences in planning and interactive decision making between experienced and inexperienced teachers. *Research Quarterly for Exercise and Sport,* **56**(1), 45-53.

Imwold, C.H., & Hoffman, S.J. (1983). Visual recognition of a gymnastic skill by experienced and inexperienced instructors. *Research Quarterly for Exercise and Sport,* **54**(2), 149-155.

Vickers, J.N. (1990). *Instructional design for teaching physical activities.* Champaign, IL: Human Kinetics Publishers.

Suggested Readings

Chyzowych, W. (1979). *The official soccer book of the United States Soccer Federation*. New York: Rand McNally.

Henshaw, R. (1979). *The encyclopedia of world soccer*. Washington, DC: New Republic Books.

Luxbacher, J., & Klein, G. (1983). *The soccer goalkeeper: A guide for players and coaches*. Champaign, IL: Leisure Press.

Luxbacher, J. (1986). *Soccer: Winning techniques*. Dubuque: Eddie Bowers Publishing Company.

Luxbacher, J. (1987). *Fun games for soccer training*. Champaign, IL: Human Kinetics Publishers.

McArdle, W., Katch, F., & Katch, V. (1981). *Exercise physiology*. Philadelphia: Lea & Febiger.

About the Author

Joseph A. Luxbacher is a former professional player in the North American Soccer League (NASL), the American Soccer League (ASL), and the Mjor Indoor Soccer League (MISL). he coaches varsity soccer at the University of Pittsburgh and holds an "A" coaching license of the United States Soccer Federation. Dr. Luxbacher serves as a consultant at soccer camps and clinics throughout the eastern United States and is a codirector of Keystone Soccer Kamps. He has addressed various national and regional conventions, including The Olympic Symposium for Coaches, and has published articles on health and fitness, nutrition, outdoor recreation, and sport psychology and sport sociology.

Dr. Luxbacher holds a doctorate in health, physical, and recreation education and has published five previous books, including *Soccer: Steps to Success, The Soccer Goalkeeper,* and *Fun Games for Soccer Training.* In his leisure, he enjoys tennis, hiking, and photography.